Why Architects Still Draw

Why Architects Still Draw

**Two Lectures
on Architectural
Drawing**

———

Paolo Belardi

translated by Zachary Nowak

THE MIT PRESS
CAMBRIDGE, MASSACHUSETTS
LONDON, ENGLAND

© 2014 Massachusetts Institute of Technology

These essays were originally published in Italian by Casa Editrice Librìa (Melfi),
as two separate volumes: *Brouillons d'Architects: una lezione sul disegno
inventivo* (2004) and *Nulla dies sine linea: una lezione sul disegno
conoscitivo* (2012).

MIT Press books may be purchased at special quantity discounts for business or
sales promotional use. For information, please email special_sales@mitpress.mit.edu.

This book was set in Utopia Std and Helvetica Neue Pro by the MIT Press.
Printed and bound in the United States of America.

Library of Congress Cataloging-in-Publication Data

Belardi, Paolo, author.
[Essays. Selections. English]
Why architects still draw / by Paolo Belardi ; translated by Zachary Nowak.
    p. cm.
Essays in English, translated from the Italian.
Includes bibliographical references and index.
ISBN 978-0-262-52548-0 (pbk. : alk. paper)
1. Architectural drawing. 2. Architectural design. 3. Drawing—Philosophy.
4. Architecture—Philosophy. I. Nowak, Zachary, translator. II. Belardi, Paolo.
Brouillons d'architects. English. III. Belardi, Paolo. Nulla dies sine linea. English.
IV. Title. V. Title: Thinking by hand. VI. Title: No day without a line.
NA2700.B428   2014
720.28′4—dc23
2013018084

10 9 8 7 6 5 4 3 2

A Federica e Angelica

Contents

Thinking by Hand: A Lecture on Inventive Drawing

No Day Without a Line: A Lecture on Informed Drawing

Translator's Note: Why *Disegno* and *Rilievo* in
Italian Mean Something More than "Drawing"
and "Survey" in English

As often happens in shifting between two languages, the words
that seem the easiest to translate are often the hardest ones
to find an adequate translation for. In this book architect-
poet Paolo Belardi makes a passionate case for why architects
should continue to draw and make surveys. The book takes
the form of two imaginary lectures to architecture students.
The first lecture is about drawings, the second about surveys.
Though both words are only seven letters long in Italian, they
were exceedingly difficult to translate, and a word about both
is necessary.

In the first lecture, "Thinking by Hand," Belardi discusses
what he calls *disegno*. This word would make anyone who
doesn't know Italian think "design," which is unfortunately
wrong. It's an example of what translators call "false friends,"
foreign words that look like English words but mean something else. *Disegno* in Italian means a drawing or a sketch, not
"design." Despite this linguistic fact, Belardi argues that the two
words should indeed be considered cousins, if not fraternal
twins. The drawing, argues Belardi, recalls the paradox of the
acorn. An acorn gives us just the barest outlines of the tree
our grandchildren might see. We can imagine the shape of its
leaves and the color of its bark, but all the other possibilities of
that future oak tree—how fast it grows, how its branches spread,
how long it lives—are to be determined. And yet that little nut

holds, inside of its shell, the whole tree already: the mature, magnificent, hundred-foot-tall oak is already "planned" within the acorn's DNA.

So too with a drawing. Even a sketch done on the back of a matchbox (to give a preview of one of Belardi's examples) can contain what will become the complete set of blueprints of the finished building. Despite its size (a matchbox in this case), the imprecision of its strokes (given the awkward surface), and its impermanence (most sketches are considered preparatory by their authors, and not saved), the sketch is like an acorn. The roughest drawing is inchoate (in the sense that it is not finished but still in evolution) and forgiving of future changes—and yet at the same time it is also, paradoxically, the entire final design. Belardi's first lecture, then, is about the magic of drawing. The author gives us examples not only from architecture but also from literature, chemistry, music, archaeology, art, and several other disciplines to show how drawing is not simply a passive act but rather a moment of invention, pregnant with creative possibilities.

The second lecture, "No Day Without a Line," is about what in Italian is called a *rilievo architettonico*. The most obvious translation for the first word is "survey," and any English speaker can then shift "architettonico" before the noun, leaving her with "architectural survey." At one time or another, all of us have likely seen what architects work with every day, the three canonic architectural views of some building made of white stone: plan, section, and elevation. These representations, apparently the output of an enormous slice-and-draw machine, give us measurements in the *x*, *y*, and *z* axes. Belardi argues that it's important—especially in today's world—to add a fourth dimension, *time*, and even a fifth one, *culture*.

A *rilievo architettonico* is the architectural equivalent of what anthropologist Clifford Geertz called a "thick description," an ethnographic approach in which the resulting text describes a group's ceremonies not only as they would understand them, but as even those unfamiliar with the group could understand them. Belardi, in "No Day Without a Line," shows how surveying a piazza cannot simply mean measuring the space and committing its width, height, and depth to paper or to an AutoCAD file. To truly know the piazza, the architectural surveyor must make an informed survey, must bring knowledge with him. How are the entrances to the open space the result of traffic patterns from centuries past? How can changing demographics and concern for environmental impacts shape the future of the piazza? What does Italian culture need from the piazza? A survey then becomes a document that relates historical details and communal needs, not just meters or feet, stone or steel.

As much as the architectural survey of the Italian tradition draws on the past, and as much as Belardi pleads the case of the pencil's relevance in "the era of the 3D scanner and the GPS device," this is not a Luddite tract. Belardi does not want us to give up high tech for watercolors or a measuring tape, and he's cognizant of the fact that any such plea would be in vain. Instead—continuing a tradition started with the "guerrilla surveyors" who so infuriated the architectural establishment in the 1970s when they "surveyed" Las Vegas's Strip with cameras and microphones—he warns us that we cannot be stuck in the past. We have to be sure that technology is the vehicle of architectural progress toward the future, and that we are the drivers. The power and precision of modern instruments push us to reduce a survey to taking precise measurements, when in fact (and Belardi surprises the reader with his eminently logical examples) metric precision is *not* the most important variable in a survey.

In addition, this book calls architects to task for their perennial obsession with canonical monuments of the past and with the same few signature glass-and-steel buildings that appear over and over in the pages of glossy magazines. Belardi argues that architectural surveys can no longer be concerned only with National Theaters, Capitol Buildings, and other Monumental Places when the real problems to be solved are not the millionth elevation of the Coliseum but rather the *banlieues* in Paris or Rome's *borgate*—the decaying outlying areas of the world's metropolises. The fourth and fifth dimensions (history and culture) that Italian architectural surveys have always included are not only relevant to today's architecture; they are necessary.

This book is about two words and what they mean—not in the sense of what their translations are, but rather what larger ideas they signify. Paolo Belardi patiently lays out his arguments that *disegno* (drawing) means more than tracing lines on a piece of paper, and that *rilievo* (surveying) means more than cross-sections and elevations. *Disegno* (drawing) means being open to all the possibilities that a pencil has concentrated in its tip, thousands of brainstorms calmed and distilled into a fraction of an ounce of graphite. *Rilievo* (surveying), on the other hand, means an informed architecture that draws on the traditions of centuries ago and the cultural realities of the present, to move architecture out of coffee table books and into the lives of those who live and work in unautographed buildings every day. That is what these two words have meant in the past, and what they still mean in the present. Belardi argues that only thinking by hand with *disegno* and using all five dimensions of the *rilievo* can make the word "architecture" mean something in the future.

For illustrations of the buildings and places discussed in this book, please visit http://pinterest.com/whyarchitects/.

Introduction: Why Architects Still Draw

In his "Life of Paolo Uccello," written in 1550, Giorgio Vasari tells us that the artist would stay in his study until late at night "seeking to solve the problems of perspective." Even when his wife would call him to come to bed, he would continue to draw, whispering in ecstasy, "Oh, what a sweet thing is this perspective!" Whether it's actually true or not, this anecdote has taken its place in the annals of history because of Vasari's approval of Uccello's late-night practice: he ends his biography of Uccello saying that it was thanks to the artist's sleepless nights that the art of prospective became "dear and useful to those who exercised themselves therein after his time," from Piero della Francesca to Leonardo da Vinci, thus permanently linking the study and practice of drawing with the idea of devotion. Perhaps it's precisely to demonstrate this connection that, after thirty years of teaching and research, I'm now developing a network of trusted collaborators with whom to share and exchange views on the future of drawing, though without the presumption of having the last word.

With my colleagues and students in mind, I've written two imaginary lectures which in reality I've never delivered (though they draw on courses I have taught at the University of Perugia). Why *do* architects still draw? These lectures are a sort of didactic canvas on which I've spread both my passion and knowledge to try to answer this question in a meaningful way. The first lecture is for students of an imagined course called "Automatic Drawing," and it poses questions about the fate of drawing by hand in the age of electronic media, and especially about the role of sketching as an interface between thought and work in the initial phase of a project. The second lecture is for students in another made-up course, "Architectural Survey." There I've explored the meaning of measurement in the era of the 3D scanner and the GPS device, trying to show the sterility of techniques that privilege metric exactitude over cultural appropriateness.

I don't know whether the references I've used here are pertinent or the rhetorical organization is orthodox. I do know, however, that my aim in both lectures is not in vain: that, even in the digital age, drawing will maintain its role as a cornerstone of architecture, reaching an even more privileged position as a way of thinking in both the creative and the informed act.

It is not by chance that this text—while peppered with quotes and iconographic allusions—doesn't have many footnotes or, more importantly, any images. This strategy was chosen deliberately to emulate the evocative tone of those old cliffhangers that relied on the reader's imagination to conjure up vivid pictures of the characters and to embellish the narratives. I care about the fate of drawing-as-thought, and I'm disturbed by writing in which the futility of expression drives readers to immediately seek solace in something besides the text. As time passes, and I see more and more writing of this kind, I am reminded of William Wordsworth's admonition:

Avaunt this vile abuse of pictured page!
Must eyes be all in all, the tongue and ear
Nothing? Heaven keep us from a lower stage!

Thinking by Hand: A Lecture on Inventive Drawing

1
Praising the Pencil

I would be lying if I said that all these poems were written with a pencil.
But I dare and love to think that nobody will want to see this title
for my poems ["Poems Written with a Pencil"] as bizarre and useless.
They really deserved to be and to stay written in pencil: if nothing
else, the gray of the thin pencil would have given them a color and
an expression.

Marino Moretti[1]

Paging through the notebooks kept by Tomaso Buzzi to direct the workers at the construction site of Buzzinda (the mysterious postmodern city erected inside the Franciscan convent of Scarzuola, halfway between Rome and Florence) is like tracing the inventive act in the process of being born. These notebooks contain page after page of the most bizarre figures taking shape: first drafted, then reworked, and in the end sketched in a final notebook, but still provisional. The *Sketches and Doodles* (as Buzzi affectionately called his notebooks) are sometimes dark, sometimes hard to comprehend, almost magical: much like Cinderella's magic pumpkin, these sketches become real, live blueprints destined for translation into structure.

This has been and remains the power of inventive drawing: to condense in a few square inches (or even less) a lot of information—and infinite possibilities. "With what words, O Writer, will you describe with like perfection the entire configuration which the drawing here does?" asks Leonardo da Vinci tendentiously, accentuating the rivalry between pen and pencil.

1. Marino Moretti, *Poesie scritte col lapis* (Naples: Ricciardi, 2010), 1.

Though, if we look closely, there isn't any real competition or conflict between writing and drawing. Take for example the letters drawn by the architect Giò Ponti and the stories painted by the writer Dino Buzzati. I've always been charmed by the rhetorical finesse with which the great poet Marino Moretti attributes the fragility of the written word to the ephemeral nature of the pencil.

This is perhaps because I sense many similarities between the regret for modernity's indifference to traditional values—in which poetry has always been rooted—and the nostalgia which many people associate with the slow evolution of the drawing instruments: from ruling pens to airbrushes, from sliding rules to Letraset sheets. If you grew up with these tools of the trade, as I did, it's easy to look with distrust at the spectacular representative virtuosities that graphic software allows. Or perhaps it's because the pencil has played a crucial role in my education—as it continues to do, if only as a memento of an almost-vanished artisan's world.

I remember the grocer of my childhood: he would sing out by heart the groceries' quantities ("three hundred grams of Parmesan cheese, one hundred grams of prosciutto, two hundred of lard ..."). Suddenly, with a speed that was every bit as good as Billy the Kid's, he would brandish the unfailing pencil stub—gnawed yet always pointed—unsheathed from his ear (its quiver) and add up the bill directly on paper. I would see this same solemnity in the blacksmith or the carpenter.

This is why I was happy when the "death of the pencil," proclaimed in the early 1990s by Alan Fletcher on the pages of the magazine *Domus*, never came. That cover, now part of the history of drawing, in addition to swarming with colored pencils (each different from the next, and all of them worn down), featured the headline "Technological Graveyard" and the subtitle "The arrival of the computer will render the pencil as useless as the stylus." "Ceci tuera cela" ("This will kill that; the printed book will destroy the building"), Victor Hugo would have said. But just as the paper page didn't destroy the stone building, the plastic mouse hasn't killed the wooden pencil.

It's not a coincidence that even in the last twenty years many people have felt anxious when faced with a blank page: they didn't have a computer, but they picked up a pencil. Or perhaps they had a tablet and they picked up a stylus for it, which is something else altogether. By virtue of its physicality (like the creative department in an ad agency), the pencil combines the individual impulsivity of the rough draft with the choral passion of brainstorming. In any event, only a great poet like Paolo Coelho could imagine that this physicality could become the pretext for moral uplift, as in his book *Like the Flowing River*:

> A boy was watching his grandmother write a letter. At one point he asked: "Are you writing a story about what we've done? Is it a story about me?"
>
> His grandmother stopped writing her letter and said to her grandson: "I am writing about you, actually, but more important than the words is the pencil I'm using. I hope you will be like this pencil when you grow up."
>
> Intrigued, the boy looked at the pencil. It didn't seem very special. "But it's just like any other pencil I've ever seen!"

"That depends on how you look at things. It has five qualities which, if you manage to hang on them, will make you a person who is always at peace with the world.

"First quality: you are capable of great things, but you must never forget that there is a hand guiding your steps. We call that hand God, and He always guides us according to His will.

"Second quality: now and then, I have to stop writing and use a sharpener. That makes the pencil suffer a little, but afterwards, he's much sharper. So you, too, must learn to bear certain pains and sorrows, because they will make you a better person.

"Third quality: the pencil always allows us to use an eraser to rub out any mistakes. This means that correcting something we did is not necessarily a bad thing; it helps to keep us on the road to justice.

"Fourth quality: what really matters in a pencil is not its wooden exterior, but the graphite inside. So always pay attention to what is happening inside you.

"Finally, the pencil's fifth quality: it always leaves a mark. In just the same way, you should know that everything you do in life will leave a mark, so try to be conscious of that in your every action."[2]

It's an unusual elegy, but not an unfounded one, because the aura of the pencil has existed since its almost apocryphal beginnings. On 10 September 1564, a violent storm pummeled the small English city of Borrowdale and ripped up an age-old tree, digging out a huge crater. In the bottom there was a vein of graphite; the local shepherds immediately saw the utility of this new dark gray mineral, but they didn't see its full potential.

2. Paolo Coelho, *Like the Flowing River*, trans. Margaret Jull Costa (New York: HarperCollins, 2006), 12–13.

They simply wrapped it up in a piece of cloth and used it to mark their herds. In any event, we know the German cabinet-maker Kaspar Faber was the first person to make pencils on a large scale, but we don't know who first had the genial idea of putting a piece of graphite between two pieces of wood. That has been lost to history.

We don't know who invented it, but the everyday pencil (just a cylinder of wood with a bit of graphite in the middle) is an extraordinary object of design: it more than merited winning Bruno Munari's "Golden Compass for the Unknown Designer." It deserved the award too because, in addition to its aesthetic virtues, it also has an amazing ethical power.

The creative synthesis of the sketch (the perfect expression of the virtuosity of the pencil) intimately joins the inventive act of the artist with the inventive act of the scientist, nullifying the separation between creation and discovery. Look at the multicolored drafts that Yves Saint Laurent, on his African safari, did for his famous Safari jackets, or the quickly traced tree of life that Charles Darwin made on his return from the Galápagos, the one that laid out the fundamental principles of evolution.

2
Writing Is Just Drawing

We're now well into the third millennium. Though reaching and moving beyond the year 2000—a symbolic and therefore meaningful goal—doesn't seem to have aroused particular emotions yet, I've decided to start with the Italian writer Italo Calvino's book *Six Memos for the Next Millennium*, selecting one particular aspect of drawing (out of the many possible) and situating it around the year 2000. As its subtitle indicates, I'm going to dedicate this first lecture to inventive drawing, which I'll do by making reference (without any distinctions) to all human activities that use sketched notes in the creative process.

This lecture takes as a starting point the exhibition "Brouillons d'écrivains" (Writers' rough drafts), set up in the spring of 2001 at Paris's Bibliothèque Nationale de France and dedicated to writers' drafts: those first drafts that, imprisoning the author's soul, sing an ode to tiny abrasions, ambiguous scratching, angry pangs. They are as messy as indecipherable notepads, though they lay the psyche bare. In a world increasingly characterized by the indirect production of images, drafts constitute the last piece of an umbilical cord to authenticity. Beyond the close relationship between writing and drawing (according to Manlio Brusatin, "writing is nothing but drawing"), there are many overlaps between Gustave Flaubert's magma-made-from-paper (from which, given his endless search for the "right" phrase, only a few words survive) and Francesco Borromini's exploded views of moldings, in which the chosen version is marked with the words "this one."

Also notable are the analogies between the pen that cuts like a razor (like that with which Victor Hugo deprived Cosette of one Jean Préjan in *Les Misérables*, renaming him Jean Valjean) and the nervous stroke with which Bramante, drawing on an idea that Giuliano da Sangallo had proposed to Pope Julius II for the construction of St. Peter's basilica, scratched out the old central-plan scheme in favor of a longitudinal one. In this sense, the pencil (even more than the pen) is an indulgent tool that not only permits inaccuracies—if not outright errors—but also allows eraser marks (never definitive) to fade away. Once again I think of the similarity between the heavily corrected pages of Carlo Emilio Gadda and the preparatory cartoons of Raffaello Sanzio, where the stroke (even if it flows impetuously) betrays a cloud of afterthoughts.

I'm aware too that my reflections might appear fragmentary, not to say disorganized. Nevertheless, I would like to try to present these reflections, passing them on as the ideal Eucharist for the new millennium, in which you will not just be technicians but also, I hope, cultured people. To put these reflections in order, as any serious lecture should in its introduction, I'm going to break my topic down into four separate parts and then a final reflection. First, I'll analyze the current situation by putting representation in long-term context so that the inherent design possibilities of drawing are clear. Second, I'll address the problem of "the beginning": how, when, and why ideas arise. Third, I'll take a short digression to talk about the underlying neurological causes and psychological motives for drawing. Fourth, I'll outline the qualities of sketching, highlighting the reasons why, even in the digital age, this particular graphic technique is still the point of origin of creation. Finally, I'll attempt to draw some conclusions.

3
Find First, Seek Later

This past millennium has been eventful for the field of drawing, witnessing the operative and theoretical acceptance of perspective and, later, the scientific consecration of descriptive geometrical methods that are used to this day. The needs of mathematics, though, ended up draining the original symbolic meaning of authority, neglecting every other pictographic narrative. It has also been the millennium of printing, and the spread of the different forms of iconic reproduction has played a crucial role in the evolution of drawing from both a cultural standpoint (the Renaissance treatises, nineteenth-century textbooks, and even today's omnipresent advertising) and an operative standpoint (the practical advantages offered by photocopiers or, more recently, scanners and smart phones). Above all, however, the second millennium was characterized by exponential technological development that deeply influenced instruments and consequently academic content.

It's obvious, for instance, that the tendency to unhinge the classic architectural walled box has to be related to the desire to conquer the third dimension, and even the fourth one (time): from Piero della Francesca's *Flagellazione* to Tintoretto's *Trasporto del corpo di San Marco* to Picasso's *Les Demoiselles d'Avignon*. This aspiration was only fully realized in the twentieth century: first by the camera, then the cinema, and (at the beginning of the 1980s) by the personal computer. Now, as Peter Eisenman once prophesied, we live in a universe of electronic media, and terms such as "microchip" and "cyberspace" have become part of our everyday lexicon. In the future, we'll likely wear electronic prostheses, and, like the main character of a famous "dream" of Akira Kurosawa who found himself submerged inside a Van Gogh piece, we'll sail through our project and directly shape its virtual simulacrum, downloading from the web sensorial fictions able to replace every type of experience: visual, aural, and tactile. This is not science fiction because, as those of you "born with the computer" know very well, we can already conjure up an object-to-be, generating it electronically in three dimensions and animating it with specific software.

Despite the extraordinary scenario envisioned above, my belief in drawing's utility for design is based on the solidity of its roots, its genetic code. Since the dawn of civilization, "drawing" has not merely meant "reproducing." Instead, as Paul Gauguin understood ("I close my eyes to see"), it means probing our internal world. To use Paul Valéry's example, in the middle of a countryside, where a philosopher foresees concepts, a geologist will only notice crystallization, a soldier will only perceive obstacles to his march, and a farmer will only envision profits. In other words, each person will tend to interpret the same system of forms and colors based on his or her own subjectivity. It's worth it then to establish some of drawing's fundamental "values," and to preserve them in the digital age. This is an era in which, paradoxically, we're attempting to regain those manual abilities that, thanks to our particular prehensile condition, characterized the appearance of *Homo sapiens* more than fifty thousand years ago.

Some early signals of what is to come have already been received. Francesco Cellini, for example, during an important recent guest lecture at the Academy of Fine Arts of Perugia, revealed that, in the academic context of architecture and engineering faculties, we have been contributing to a phenomenon that was unpredictable until a few years ago. There is a desire among those of the new generation to regain a relationship with materiality, to get dirty when working with objects, to go back to actual sculptural modeling and manual drawing exercises. Perhaps this desire is motivated by the material component of design, which entails a direct experience somehow bordering on biological necessity.

To strengthen the relationship that has always linked the two contrasting concepts, "drawing" and "[working] project," until the two converge into that almost indissoluble unit called a work of architecture, we can reflect on the two terms' etymologies. Often linguistic analysis clarifies ambiguities. The tight connections between "drawing" and "project" are exemplified in Anglo-Saxon culture by the use of the word "design," which, like the Italian *disegno*, has its etymological roots in the Latin word *designare*. This verb's most archaic meaning is "to represent," in the simple verb *signare*, meaning "to mark," "to trace," "to establish," "to express," and—most importantly of all—with the prefix *de*, an intensifier of "an action to take place, a high level of something." Therefore, the meaning of "designer" originally coincides with that of "designator," in other words "he who chooses after having given meaning to things."

At this point, the relationship between "design" and "project" seems to be an affinity, which becomes an identity at the moment we realize that the term "design"—*disegno* in Italian—means a purpose, a specific program, a "project." Above all, this drawing/project unity becomes clear when, as I intend to do in this lecture, we try to trace the dynamics of that creative act which philosophers call "heuristics." Here again it's worthwhile to look at the word's roots: "heuristics" comes from the Greek verb ευρισκω, which does not originally mean "to discover" but rather "to find." Jean Cocteau understood this well, hence his mantra "Find first, seek later." Thus heuristics was originally an interpretive activity, aimed at making some implicit possibilities (often hidden by a mystifying appearance) explicit. One might define an inventor as a person who, as Viktor Shklovsky said, "is able to detach the object from the usual associations."

An inventor then is a person who can create new combinations out of their cognitive heritage, something Henri Poincaré called "unpredictable connections." Nothing can be created from nothing, and what is useful must also be innovative. Fra Angelico was inventive when hitting upon that particular blue tone that characterizes his skies, which he made by mixing the rarefied blue of Siena's tradition with the more intense blue that Giotto had used in Assisi. Le Corbusier was just as inventive when he came up with an apartment building-viaduct for Rio de Janeiro by combining two apparently disparate suggestions: the car test track on top of a Fiat factory in Turin designed by Giacomo Mattè Trucco and the arcades of ancient aqueducts in the Roman countryside.

In the heuristic act, memory is the future of the past, especially if it is urged on by randomness: from the submerged body for Archimedes to the lamp that oscillated in Pisa's cathedral for Galileo Galilei, from the apple that fell from the tree for Isaac Newton to the water cans of "sora Cesarina" for Enrico Fermi. Getting back to architecture, we can think of Aldo Rossi, who, when visiting an osteological museum, was so impressed with the structural analogies between animal bones and archaeological ruins that he "dramatized" the plan for Modena's cemetery, making it resemble a backbone.

You who have chosen a profession that aims to modify the status quo are aware of this: a project is always, at the beginning, a "riddle," a complicated problem with apparently irresolvable constraints (e.g., a more powerful engine is also heavier) and held back by the respect for rules that limit the possible solutions. For example, a cable-stayed bridge, besides being stable in wind gusts and obeying highway standards, must also follow environmental protection laws. A project, precisely because it's a bearer of novelty, must solve contradictions and follow rules—its novelty is the "new" application of an existing rule, the extension of an existing rule to a "new" context, or the institution of a "new" rule.

Not just that: given that the rules in architecture are as numerous as they are different—we can think here of certain "laws" (static laws, hygienic/sanitary codes, morphologic influences, etc.) and cultural aspirations (ethical, philosophic, aesthetic, etc.)—the architect's puzzle becomes a sort of arbitration among the different viewpoints, each with various dimensions. Finally, a creative action must be triggered for the possible-to-actual transition to occur; an action that is not merely abstract but rather "competent and aware of the objective," as the theorist of problem solving Genrich Altshuller says. ¹³

4
Ideas Are in the Air

While discussing the problem of how ideas arise in his *Science of Logic*, Hegel stated that "the beginning must be an absolute, or what is synonymous here, an abstract beginning." Therefore, a new beginning "may not suppose anything, must not be mediated by anything ... it must be purely and simply an immediacy, or rather merely immediacy itself."[3] In other words, Hegel declares the utter necessity of intuition, renouncing the control of the rational mind in favor of unconscious foresight. This is perhaps motivated by the fact that self-censoring doesn't exist in the unconscious or in ideas, which, redeemed from the legacy of "functional fixity," are free to combine in improbable and ever-mixing associations.

There are many paradigms of the inventive act, but Graham Wallas's 1921 theory is still particularly interesting today. Wallas, though aware of the fluidity of the creative process, subdivided it into four phases. The first phase, *preparation*, consists of focusing on the problem, realizing that it can be solved, and collecting and organizing the required information.

---

3. Georg Wilhelm Friedrich Hegel, *Science of Logic*, trans. A. V. Miller (Atlantic Highlands, NJ: Humanities Press International, 1989), §99.

The second phase, *incubation*, concerns the manipulation of the collected material not only via sequential reasoning but also through mental feedback circuits. These two phases together are called "maturation," which might last for years—even thirty years in the case of Andrew Wiles's demonstration of Fermat's Last Theorem. The third phase, *illumination*, is concentrated on the epiphany of the solution, and ignores all hierarchies in activating all possible thinking modes: deduction, induction, and abduction. The fourth and final phase, *validation*, focuses on the logical structure of what has been elaborated so as to make the idea comprehensible, communicable, and feasible. As a result, there is a significant difference between the third phase and the others in terms of both time and intellectual importance, exemplified by Thomas Edison's belief that "genius is one percent inspiration and ninety-nine percent perspiration."

Wallas underrated two crucial aspects, though. First, he didn't give enough importance to the role of the cultural context, which is particularly relevant for the initial point of departure. From Pericles' Athens to Federico da Montefeltro's Urbino to Maria Theresa's Vienna: imagine how important it was to be born and educated in those precise historical periods, rather than in a nomad camp or the Siberian steppe. Most critically, though, Wallas didn't investigate the methods of enlightenment enough, omitting a critical analysis of the always-present conditions of inventive genesis. Although it's not my intention to reduce creativity to an algorithm, let's try to list these conditions that are always present, documenting them with examples.

Ideas arise from fortuitous circumstances. According to legend, Charles Didelot, *maître de ballet* and choreographer at London's King's Theater, was the first to experiment with the use of *en pointe* (tiptoe) ballet position in his *Zéphir and Flore* in 1804. It is also interesting that this innovation was suggested by a mechanical system, created to lift the prima ballerina and let her "fly" in a circle above the stage. Just before the mechanical lifting, the dancer was hooked to the winch through multiple invisible wires; the ability to dance in this position facilitated the gradual adoption of the technique of "dancing en pointe"— later named the *aérien* style by Maria Taglioni.

Ideas arise from observations that are outside of their specific field. The autobiographies of Francis Crick and James Watson, who in 1953 discovered DNA's double helix structure, described their lengthy research. It was carried out atom by atom in a scenario in which hopes and disappointments alternated, occupying months and months of exhausting calculations, mockup constructions, and chemical manipulations— all without any success. Unexpectedly, the scientists intuited DNA's spatial organization in a Cambridge cinema room while watching a scene in Robert Siodmak's *The Spiral Staircase* in which the camera was held above a spiral staircase, exaggerating its cyclical shape. Crick and Watson left the cinema and ran back to the Cavendish Laboratory, confirming shortly thereafter that the spiral geometry was indeed correct, a perfect match.

Ideas arise in the most disparate places. Roland Barthes, for example, preferred the train to the airplane as a place more conducive to invention, whereas French anthropologist Marc Augé maintains that the bicycle is the means of transport most suited to concentrating and having new ideas. Virginia Woolf loved to daydream about novel plots while enjoying a hot bath, whereas Wayne Silby isolated himself inside a room for sensorial deprivation each time he had to solve financial problems.

Ideas can arise at any moment. Wassily Kandinsky, for instance, used to paint only during the day and with incredible regularity. Honoré de Balzac loved to compose with a clear mind, waking up at sunrise, while Antoine Lavoisier preferred to work at night.

Ideas arise from boredom. During a conference on film in Assisi in 1962, Italian director Pier Paolo Pasolini got bored and started absentmindedly flipping through a copy of the Gospel of Matthew. He was struck with how the world of the farmer in the age of Christ was documented in a text that was important not only for its religious fervor but also for its realistic brutality. This inspired the amazing shots of his film *La ricotta* and, later, the revolutionary shots of *Il Vangelo secondo Matteo*. Likewise, J. K. Rowling, author of the popular Harry Potter series, got the idea for her main character during an excruciatingly long train trip on the Manchester-London route, during which she was thinking of her childhood friend Ian Potter.

Ideas arise from oversights. Antoine de Saint-Exupéry, in *The Wisdom of the Sands*, highlights the importance of what he calls a "fertile mistake." The author talks about creation sometimes being a misstep, sort of like hitting the chisel wrong on the stone, but with a positive (if unexpected) result. In the

same way, Alberto Savinio would always talk about the importance of the misprint as bearer of the unexpected, encouraging
others to give what seemed like an error a second chance, as
some of them turn out successful. Ideas arise when one is lost
in thought, making automatic movements. Nolan Bushnell got
the inspiration for *Space Invaders*—the first successful video-
game—while letting grains of sand flow through his fingers.
The realist painter Grant Wood, to get his inspiration back,
used to abandon his brushes to milk the cows on his ranch.

Ideas arise from habit. As everyone knows, Immanuel
Kant's philosophic speculations were written at mechanical
times and with ritual gestures. Fewer people know that Richard
Wagner was able to finish the third act of *Tristan und Isolde*
only thanks to eating some food that had been prohibited
by his doctors. He was served a little plate of milk toast and
it made him realize what he was missing, and why he hadn't
been able to write a note for eight days.

Ideas arise from necessity. Jacob Schick, bedridden because
of a twisted ankle while stationed in Alaska, realized that the
Gillette razor was not practical enough and began to work on
a dry razor with its own engine. Schick reached his goal in 1923,
and took out a patent on the first electric razor.

Ideas arise from serendipity, when looking for something
completely different. The accidental discovery of penicillin
by Alexander Fleming is a classic example of serendipity, but
another one that shows how important it is to interpret something correctly is provided by the American astronomer James
Christy. In 1978 Christy was observing Pluto's orbit, using a "star

scanner" into which he could insert a planet's picture to measure it. He saw that in the image he had chosen, Pluto seemed to be squished, though with a definite protuberance. He attributed this fact to the low-quality picture and decided to change it.

18

Fate intervened, however. The scanner jammed and Christy needed the help of a technician, who took two hours to fix the instrument. During this time, Christy's eyes came to see the deformation differently, and that photo, which he had first chalked up to error, became an obsession. While waiting for the technician, the astronomer looked through the photographic archives on Pluto and found an example marked "Pluto image elongated." Flipping through the years between 1965 and 1970, he found six other similar pictures, confirming his intuition: the photo was correct and showed something that nobody had ever noticed before. The elongations were because Pluto had a moon, Charon.

Ideas arise from dreams. The most famous such episode concerns Friedrich August Kekulé von Stradonitz. In the middle of the nineteenth century, Kekulé's dedication to his research on the structural form of benzene was so intense that he often fell into trances in which images of dancing atoms appeared. In 1856, late one afternoon after hours of attempting to solve the problem, he fell asleep in front of his fireplace. To describe what happened next, I'll cite Kekulé's report verbatim:

> I was sitting writing on my textbook, but the work did not progress; my thoughts were elsewhere. I turned my chair to the fire and dozed. Again the atoms were gamboling before my eyes. This time the smaller groups kept modestly in the background. My mental eye, rendered more acute by the repeated visions of the kind,

could now distinguish larger structures of manifold conformation; long rows sometimes more closely fitted together all twining and twisting in snake-like motion. But look! What was that? One of the snakes had seized hold of its own tail, and the form whirled mockingly before my eyes. As if by a flash of lightning I awoke; and this time also I spent the rest of the night in working out the consequences of the hypothesis.[4]

This time, the work was successful: the snake's image had suggested the ring structure of the benzene molecule to Kekulé. No less evocative is the story of Giuseppe Tarantini, whose *Sonata per violino in sol minore*, known as *Trillo del diavolo*, is said to have been inspired by a violinist with Mephistophilesque features. Think too of James Watt, who, after a nightmare in which he was hit by a marble, invented a new method to produce the lead cones for bullets.

We could keep going, making this list long enough to be impractical for our purposes (our list certainly does not exhaust the subject), because ways that enlightenment arises—a hybrid mix of intentions, chance, and attentions—elude every form of cataloging. Nevertheless, this variety of situations proves that, as Andy Warhol suggested, "ideas are in the air," viral elements ready to be assimilated by the most sensitive souls. Louis Pasteur used to admonish his students, "Fortune favors the mind that is prepared," to which Daniel Goleman added, "and passionate." It is not by chance that Erwin Schrödinger, the 1933 Nobel Prize winner in physics and the father of wave mechanics, wrote in his diary: "I have never had a good idea without having a new girlfriend, too."

---

4. Royston M. Roberts, *Serendipity: Accidental Discoveries in Science* (New York: John Wiley and Sons, 1989), 75–81.

5
The Mind Rules over the Hand;
Hand Rules over Mind

Few research topics are as fascinating and full of possibilities as the study of the complicated mechanisms that regulate brain activity. Despite the newness of this field, the last several decades have seen remarkable progress, progress based on the shift from a mechanical to a dynamic conception of the brain, proposed by Gerald Edelman in the 1970s. While Gottfried Wilhelm Leibniz had compared the brain's structure to a mill in the seventeenth century and the analogy to the Turing machine prevailed in the mid-twentieth century, Edelman drew on and refined John Eccles's studies on conditioned reflexes.

Edelman introduced a theory of selection according to which two people's brains are never identical, even in homozygous twins, but instead even in the embryonic phase show wide ranges of variability. For Edelman, then, our world doesn't have a predefined structure; on the contrary, it is our brain that, shaping itself in response to external stimuli, creates our reality using sensory input. Sensations aren't enough, however, as they fail to account for movement. In knowledge, sensation and movement integrate with one another, creating a certain "category," a coherent response in the brain that is the antecedent of a "meaning." In addition, because successive "explorations"—i.e., sensations of the same subject in different times and contexts—are never the same, each category is determined and then reclassified an infinite number of times.

It is through this endless process of structuring/destructuring/restructuring that each person creates his or her creative aptitude. This reminds me of Miloš Forman's Mozart, who, when asked to repeat an extraordinary harpsichord improvisation, did not perform the same one but rather a new and unpredictable variation. The same goes for Louis Armstrong, who, when questioned about the uniqueness of a jazz solo, gave the example of a bird unable to land on a branch the same way twice. Thus Edelman's message is ultimately that we are not immaterial spirits fluctuating inside a machine, but rather streams of the sensations, perceptions, images, memories, reflections, corrections, and reclassifications that, in a rather haphazard and contingent way, flow inside us.

From this point of view, it's not possible to interpret the brain as an aseptic container of impersonal processes: rather, it's a confederation, an organic unit that is able to reflect on itself. Looking closely, it's precisely this capacity that is able to solder together body, brain, and mind. In addition, the recognition that the interactivity between body and brain can be investigated using the methods of classical physics allowed Roger Penrose to come up with a hypothesis on communication mechanisms between brain and mind, demonstrating that some brain processes (like conscience and consciousness) are directly connected to the physical phenomenon of "quantum coherence." This is the same mechanism that allows current-carrying electrons to move simultaneously in a coherent way in low-temperature metals, giving rise to superconductivity.

Something similar—though under very different conditions—also happens in the human brain, which is composed of billions of neurons that are in turn formed by thousands of microtubes. According to Penrose, like the electrons in superconductivity, the state of maximum "coherent excitement" of brain microtubes allows the cognitive process to occur, all of which happens very quickly, in about half a second. This quantum coherence phenomenon, besides explaining rationally the dynamics of cognitive processes, is responsible for the mind's "unitary sense" in which (according to Penrose) the conscious process is never the result of a single cortical area's activation but rather the synergistic result of numerous parts of the brain.

Paradoxically, the main consequence of the application of quantum physics—which is based upon indeterminacy and unpredictability—to the study of brain mechanisms is the introduction of a purely subjective component in the observation and measurement of brain processes. It is the person who becomes responsible for phenomena, which he or she doesn't observe or measure but simply evaluates. This has important ramifications for the complicated hand-brain relationship: the hand-related sensors in the cortex are much larger than those related to the rest of the body, and they directly affect the modalities with which our brain manages the dynamics of writing or drawing.

When editing a text, for instance, the hand might perform from four to five million small movements, which all together give rise to the marks on the paper. When we write, though, we don't have full control of our handwriting: we trace in an automatic and unconscious way, given that, during just one second of writing, our hand is subject to at least ten graphic impulses. In this way, unconscious automation related to the complicated neurological-muscle activity happens so that, as Henri Focillon maintains, "the mind rules over the hand; hand rules over mind."[5]

Beyond the various hypotheses about which particular part of the brain is responsible for the written language, some of Rudolf Pophal's research is interesting. Pophal didn't make any distinction between writing and drawing (a reminder to the reader: this was my lecture's starting point) but rather simply classified the results based on the dominance of related brain centers. In so doing, Pophal was the first to interpret the "graphic act" as a unique and nonrepeatable brain stratification.

In this holistic context, every detail, regardless of importance, is enhanced: slowness and an inclination to make something smaller reveal doubt; rapid but interrupted tracing indicates emotional anxiety; different forms of methodic inequality—precision, acceleration, and personal inclination—disclose aptitude. We might ask ourselves about the specifics of sketching, a field as mysterious as it is pregnant with fascinating ambiguities. Benjamin Libet has shown that when we trace something, especially if this is done impulsively, our brain takes 500 milliseconds to elaborate it consciously, while only 150 milliseconds are required for the unconscious sensory reception. The awareness of our graphic act, then, implies a very brief discrepancy—350 milliseconds—between what we see and what we know we have seen. What occurs during this very

5. Henri Focillon, *The Life of Forms in Art*, trans. Charles Beecher Hogan and George Kubler (New York: Zone Books, 1992), 184.

short time frame? Many details related to the elusive nature of creativity may be successfully pursued in the mental images that are evoked in this "black hole" of the drawing act.

6

Sketches Are the DNA of an Idea

In cognitive activity in general and in inventive activity in particular, the human brain proceeds by analogies rather than sequences. It collects all the information (even casual) from the exterior world and its own interiority and synthetically visualizes it with the help of that extraordinary seismograph called the hand. An idea arises as a type of sketch, or, according to the Italian linguist Giacomo Devoto's definition, "a rough draft drawn with few essential marks ... open to greater development, but able to be considered complete as well."

The sketch, then, despite often being the size of a stamp or a pack of matches, is neither the representation nor the embryo of the idea but rather, as Franco Purini said, "the DNA of ideas." It is the idea's genesis because it tends to solve, within the context of the inventive kernel of activity, every complexity of what is still outside that kernel, however temporarily. To explain myself better, and to reveal the qualities that have always characterized the "rough" (as the first bunch of marks on paper drawn by a creative person, somewhere between concept and image, are called in advertising jargon), that place where ideas are sifted, I'll use several examples as a jumping-off point. At first they'll seem unrelated to architecture, but I'll get there forthwith.

I'll start by relating what happened to Otto Loewi, a 1936 Nobel Prize winner in physiology and medicine. Loewi received this prestigious award because he demonstrated that nerve impulses are transmitted by chemical substances. In reality, Loewi had foreseen the outlines of his discovery at least twenty years prior but had not been able to demonstrate his hypothesis. Around 1930 he began doing lab experiments to prove the presence of chemical substances secreted by a frog's heart under nerve stimulus. He was unsuccessful. At this point, Loewi became very anxious and suffered insomnia. One night he was very tired and used a sedative to sleep. In the middle of the night, Loewi awoke with a vivid impression of having found the solution to his problem; he could not, however, get dressed and run off to his laboratory because he was still dizzy from the sleeping pills.

When he woke up the next day, he couldn't remember clearly the revelation he had had that night, and lost heart. Luckily, however, Loewi later recalled the solution while walking in a park. He took a business card out of his wallet and jotted down the basics of what he imagined the process was. Back in the laboratory, Loewi demonstrated in an unambiguous and repeatable way that nerves influence heartbeats, releasing a chemical substance from their terminus when stimulated. There is a similar story concerning Antonio Tabucchi, who told of having gotten the idea for his *Requiem* during a break in a Parisian bistro: "The place was empty. I suddenly remembered something, so I took my notebook (which I always carry with me) out of my pocket, because I know very well, after many years spent writing, that a story can suddenly come to you, and if you don't have the tool to catch it or at least to sketch it, it might go away as easily as it came."[6]

I would ask then if there is any difference between Terence's *Andria* text, annotated by Angelo Poliziano, which led to the Florentine rediscovery of classic theater; the studies on whirlpools glossed by Leonardo da Vinci in the Codex Hammer, studies which accelerated the union between naturalistic experimentation and the science of painting; and the sketches of Italian Renaissance palaces that emerge from Robert Venturi's memos, which anticipated postmodern irony. I don't think so, because sketching is, above all, a valuable notational system that somehow is ahead of the future.

Let's move on to the second example. Again Calvino and again *Six Memos for the Next Millennium.* In the second memo, which is dedicated to quickness, Calvino concludes by telling the story of Chuang-Tzu, a talented artist who was asked by the king to draw a crab. To do the job, Chuang-Tzu asks for five years of time and a villa with twelve servants, which the king promptly provides. After the five years the work is still not even in draft form and Chuang-Tzu asks for five more years. The king grants the extension. At the end of the ten years, Chuang-Tzu finally seizes a brush and, in front of an incredulous king, sketches a crab in an instant and with a single gesture: it was the most beautiful crab ever seen.

It's tempting to find analogies in other human activities as well, like advertising. I remember the extemporaneous sketch

6. Antonio Tabucchi, *Autobiografie altrui: Poetiche a posteriori* (Milan: Feltrinelli, 2003), 15–16.

drawn by Aldo Cernuto—creative director of Pirella Göttsche Lowe agency—during a long brainstorming session to come up with the 1997 institutional poster for Volvo Italia. This sketch communicated the Swedish automobile company's commitment to safety using the image of an intact walnut inside a crushed one. It's even easier to find analogies in architecture: there's only the difficulty of choosing among the many examples. Among the many possible, I like to think of Le Corbusier, who, during breakfast with his cousin Pierre Jeanneret in a Paris restaurant in the spring of 1923, quickly sketched on a menu those superimposed cells that, in the following years, would constitute the basic idea of his Unité d'Habitation. Unfortunately it was a sketch that history didn't preserve, though it would emerge over and over in the notebooks on the Ville Contemporaine. Le Corbusier, as Pierre would later recount, elaborated his sketch in a matter of seconds.

Because of the inherent properties of sketching, Le Corbusier concentrated into those few seconds the vast amount of knowledge and images he had accumulated during travels in his youth, including the spatial articulations of the Florence Charterhouse, which he surveyed and redrew repeatedly until he had finally internalized it. I would also like to recall the advice that my master, Vittorio de Feo, used to give to his students: "When you get an idea, don't hold it," because otherwise you risk destroying its vitality. In architecture, sketching must be used to translate an idea out of a state of mere will, especially (as often happens) if the sketch is drawn impulsively as the real-time transcription of unconsciously accumulated energy.

Sketching, because of its inherent conciseness, is therefore a notational system characterized by quickness. Third example. Gabriele D'Annunzio used to compose rhymes in his study, while standing and leaning on a lectern. The poet himself reported, however, having written his "La pioggia nel pineto" in less than fifteen minutes, noting it down on some toilet paper while sitting in the bathroom of his villa. Although he was dealing with far more prosaic physiological functions at the time, he was inspired by the sudden misty rain of that early afternoon.

Nevertheless, is D'Annunzio's toilet paper so different from André Chénier's bedsheet, on which he jotted down his last lines in the Parisian prison of Saint-Lazare before mounting the scaffold? Or what about the Miramare's hotel stationery on which Guglielmo Marconi, having suddenly woken up in the middle of the night, solved the equations for short-wave reflectors? Or from the baseball program on which Moses Pendleton—during a game—sketched a choreography for the Momix company? Isn't it the same desire to fix ideas fast that drove Saverio Muratori to draft a typological system on a tram ticket, Carlo Scarpa to jot down a construction drawing on a Swiss cigarette box, and Oswald Mathias Ungers to doodle a texture of modular patterns on a Lufthansa napkin? So we can expand the list of sketching's properties by adding, in addition to its notational character and quickness, its availability in every situation, even the most embarrassing and unusual ones.

As a fourth example, take Giacomo Leopardi's "L'infinito," perhaps his best-known, most admired, and most commented-on poem. Leopardi, like Dante Alighieri and Torquato Tasso, was as much a poet as a scientist, and all his works, which seem vague and instinctive, are actually precise and well thought out, a result of multiple revisions. Giuseppe De Robertis has analyzed the restless rewrites of "L'infinito": the original text is almost illegible because of the author's innumerable corrections, made at different times. Leopardi wrote *celeste confine* ("celestial border") instead of *ultimo orizzonte* ("last horizon"); *interminato spazio* ("endless space") as a replacement for *interminato spazi* ("endless spaces"). He vacillated between *immensitade* ("immensitude") and *infinità* ("infinity") before choosing *immensità* ("immensity").

Think of how important it was, from a compositional point of view, that Leopardi inverted *il mio pensier s'annega* ("my thought drowns") to *s'annega il pensier mio*, avoiding putting *s'annega* ("to drown") next to *naufragar* ("to be shipwrecked"), but most of all linking the concept of thought with that of sinking. "L'infinito," in its final version, is an immediate, shattering, and apparently "simple" text, though experts have written reams attempting to decipher why Leopardi changed the original draft, which is still considered a goldmine of possibilities for understanding his poetics today.

Once again, De Robertis's tenacity in decoding the poem resembles Carlo Ludovico Ragghianti's stubbornness: when working on a critical essay on Alvar Aalto's works, Ragghianti flew to Helsinki to examine the Finnish master's sketches with a magnifying glass. Architectural sketches, in fact, like Leopardi's lyrics and Luigi Nono's sheet music—well known for their illegibility given the layers of variation—are very useful for the comprehension of their authors' poetics, as they are "dense schemes," as Nelson Goodman has defined these. Such sketches reveal with their "thickness" the tortuous process of design, revealing references and images that were not strictly part of the project: ideas abandoned and then retrieved, along with uncertainties, disappointments, and enthusiasm.

Sketching is a notational system that is not only rapid and ready but also a mode of accessing information. A fifth example. As you probably know, Michelangelo Buonarroti ordered the destruction of all of his preparatory drawings after his death, demonstrating with great intellectual honesty the temporary (and therefore private) nature of sketching: not just the quick draft of a well-defined thought, but rather the more effective representation of the draft of thought. Sketching, both because of its small dimensions and indeterminacy on paper as well as its independence from any code, is able to continuously regenerate itself, always offering new suggestions—sometimes ones that prove surprising even to their author.

The sketch, then, is an "open" tool that is ready to perform a destabilizing role that, immediately after its definition, can renew itself as often as one desires—all based on an actual act of parthenogenesis. More than four centuries after Michelangelo, James Stirling, in one of his last interviews, remarked on the ephemeral character of sketching as a work in progress. According to him it's the "interaction between the designer's almost-unconscious thoughts and the sometimes-autonomous shapes of sketched marks." Exemplary, in this sense, are the sketches that Stirling developed for Electa Publishers' Venetian

pavilion: the initial reference to Hapsburg kiosks was replaced by a more contextualized suggestion that, line by line, displaced the initial reference to the kiosks and called to mind the lagoon's steamboats. Sketching thus presents itself as a quick, readily available, dense, and self-generative notational system.

A sixth and final example. When Adso and William of Baskerville first enter the abbey where the story will take place in Umberto Eco's novel *The Name of the Rose*, Adso describes it as follows:

> After the gate (which was the only opening in the outer walls), a tree-lined avenue led to the abbatial church. To the left of the avenue there stretched a vast area of vegetable gardens and, as I later learned, the botanical garden, around the two buildings of the balneary and the infirmary and herbarium, following the curve of the walls. Behind, to the left of the church, rose the Aedificium, separated from the church by a yard scattered with graves. The north door of the church faced the south tower of the Aedificium, which offered, frontally, its west tower to the arriving visitor's eyes; then, to the left, the building joined the walls and seemed to plunge, from its towers, toward the abyss, over which the north tower, seen obliquely, projected. To the right of the church there were some buildings, sheltering in its lee, and others around the cloister: the dormitory, no doubt, the abbot's house, and the pilgrims' hospice, where we were heading. We reached it after crossing a handsome flower garden. On the right side, beyond a broad lawn, along the south walls and continuing eastward behind the church, a series of peasants' quarters, stables, mills, oil presses, granaries, and cellars, and what seemed to me to be the novices' house.[7]

---

7. Umberto Eco, *The Name of the Rose*, trans. William Weaver (New York: Warner Books, 1986), 18–19.

Supposedly when the director Jean-Jaques Annaud began the cinematographic transposition of Eco's novel, he found it so difficult to reconstruct the above-described set that he asked Eco for help; the writer gave him one of his own sketches, developed during the novel's writing. In the same way, in a letter written in Italian to his friend Ernesta Pelizza Marangoni on 16 August 1946, Albert Einstein, when looking for the appropriate word, didn't hesitate to use a quick pen sketch to clarify an important concept. He wrote, "I am also happy to hear that all of the Casteggiani friends except Julia Mai's husband are fine and the dear Mussolini ... , as honestly deserved." After "dear Mussolini," he sketched a hanged puppet that unambiguously communicates his opinion of the events at Piazzale Loreto.

Getting back to architecture, it's worth mentioning the well-known epistle with which Leon Battista Alberti—wanting to instruct Matteo de' Pasti on the redesign of Rimini's Tempio Malatestiano's main facade—completes his text with a tiny sketch that, far better than any possible literal description, transmits the intention of crowning the facade with two facing volutes. Still better, how can we not think of the sketches used by the entrepreneur Frederick Robie to explain to Frank Lloyd Wright his needs in a house, or how Le Corbusier's Father Pierre Couturier illustrated a Dominican monastery's organizational distribution to him.

We can therefore conclude that *sketching is a quick, readily available, dense, self-generative, and, above all, extraordinarily communicative notational system*. The combination of these qualities, producing a sort of magic potion powered by the mental images that emerge from Libet's "black hole," makes it a precious tool for all human activities that deal with creativity: Luigi Pirandello noted the "Everybody in his own way" motto that stands out against the church bell tower in Coazze. So too Michelangelo Antonioni designed the set for the final explosion in *Zabriskie Point* with a simple floor plan, and David Bowie visualized with affected naïveté the political contents of *I'm Afraid of Americans*. Most of all, sketching technique is essential for architecture, embracing two distinct but complementary fields: one on the path of knowledge, approaching something that already exists, and the other on the path of conception, concerning what one has in mind to create.

In the first category, which includes the notes and surveys of ancient architecture and of contemporary works, travel sketches—able to capture the most intimate and subjective environmental qualities in few strokes—stand out. For instance, Louis Kahn, during his Italian grand tour, painted the stark contrast between the light and shadows of Pisa's Piazza dei Miracoli with a marked intensity, showing his taste for geometric solids. In the second category (which includes graphic precursors), theoretical sketches, able to anticipate new poetic frontiers, are particularly notable. For example, the series of sketches that Konstantin Melnikov developed for the USSR pavilion at the Paris Exposition of 1925 foreshadow deconstructivism by eradicating the modern city's symbols—the Ferris wheel, advertising signage, etc.—and reassembling them in new volumetric combinations.

Drawing and project then—though remaining different entities—nourish each other from the moment of conception on, forming a tangle of meanings that demonstrates their interdependence. Despite the inherent dimensional imprecision (in a sketch on a 1:500 scale, the soft pencil's stroke, about 1 millimeter wide, corresponds to 50 centimeters) and the independence from every type of codification (think of Mario Ridolfi's "multiple staircases"), the type of representation in sketching is in fact inseparable from the intentions of design. For instance, if Gian Lorenzo Bernini's planimetric sketch for the layout of Piazza del Quirinale in Rome controls the visual device's effectiveness, Joseph Paxton's draft blueprint of London's Crystal Palace orders the phases of construction, while Erich Mendelsohn's perspective sketch for Berlin's Woga-Komplex exalts his monumental proposal. But their contents always remain inside the disciplinary borders. Even inside evocative variations on a theme (such as Oscar Niemeyer's sketches developed by revising ideas already realized, giving them additional meanings), sketching, rather than an end-in-itself *divertissement*, is a creative tool that also requires a precise physical effort. This is clear in Carlo Aymonino's eloquent drawing in which some sketches are composed from memory around an epigraph—"designing is effort"—from which blood drips.

7
"Draw, Antonio, Draw . . ."

At this point, many threads have been interwoven in my lecture. Given the fact that the line—the basis of drawing—can reasonably be associated with an untied knot or a rope that binds, which thread must I pull so as to find the conclusion in my hands? There is the thread that holds together the whole history of representation—from *Homo sapiens* to *Homo digitalis*. There is also the thread that connects design to the other expressive activities—poetry, cinema, music, dancing—the thread that links the hand to the brain (admirably integrating conscience and corporeality), and the thread that sews up the wound opened by Carlo Aymonino.

Perhaps, though, there is neither a thread to pull nor a conclusion to reach. On the contrary, rather than leaving you with a moral, with some intellectual get-out-of-jail-free card for the electronic media age because today we're starting the Automatic Drawing course (a misleading title, inherited with excessive reverence from the world of mechanics), I would ask you to be aware of the inherent limits of computer-assisted tools. This because nothing, whether in drawings or in projects, is *automatic*: therefore you must be fully aware of the risks that go along with the new "immersive systems" and the much-praised "virtual reality." There was a movie by Emidio Greco, *Morel's Invention*, that few people have seen. It's based on Adolfo Bioy Casares's novel of the same name, and its protagonist is a fugitive who escapes from the police and lands on an island where strange events occur. The island is inhabited by a group of characters who despite having the same characteristics as real people—three-dimensional consistencies, voices, colors, smells, etc.—are mere holograms, projected by a machine designed by a diabolic scientist, Morel. After killing real people,

Morel projects their images on the island, satisfying his desire to manipulate history. Our main character has the chance to watch (though without the ability to interfere) the various characters' lives. He falls in love with one of them, Faustine, with whom he can't communicate, as she is ultimately just an image of another world, however hyperrealistic. The only way to contact his lover will be to be filmed by the machine and projected into the same space, though of course he would die in the process.

Let's get this straight: I am not going to suggest that you underrate digital tools, which are full of both inventive and communicative possibilities: you would risk not keeping up with times. However, being aware of the limits of these innovative representational techniques means avoiding confusing the means with the end. Use all available representational techniques, from a pencil to a mouse, with a pluralistic attitude that will ultimately be good for your creativity. More than a century ago a sarcastic Karl Marx, in the middle of a similar epoch-making period, was wondering about the future of the god Jupiter in the age of the lightning rod, or of Mercury in the face of Crédit Mobilier. Just so we might wonder today about the future of Diboutades or Saurias of Samos—mythic inventors of drawing—in the electronic media age. And maybe, surrendering to technological progress, we can give in to the temptation of decreeing the final death of the pencil in favor of the mouse or the cybernetic glove.

But it won't happen this way because, as Fernando Távora says, "Only if you're able to draw in a traditional way can you

also properly draw using a computer."[8] We can think of the *edili*—the "builders" in ancient Rome, who were also magistrates dedicated to the temple's safeguarding. The root of the Italian word *edile* goes back to the Greek word $\alpha\iota\theta\omega$, "lighting," "burning": so too you, as future designers (or rather as "designers of the future"), will be asked to preserve these values like the ancient vestals: indifferent to trends. Don't overlook any branch of drawing's family tree, and above all always follow the advice that Michelangelo Buonarroti gave to Antonio, an assistant who asked him about the right path to becoming a great artist. The master noted it on a piece of paper while sketching a bacchanal's putto: "Draw, Antonio, draw ..."

To make you aware of this responsibility, and to pay homage to what Calvino used to do in his lectures, I would like to leave you with a short story, borrowed from a beautiful piece of poetry. A middle-aged man enters a Gothic construction site and, approaching an architect, asks him: "What are you drawing?" The architect replies: "I am drawing a wall." Unsatisfied, the man goes over to a second architect, and repeats his question. The architect answers: "I am drawing a window." Stubbornly, the man poses the same question to a third architect. The answer is again inadequate: "I am drawing a door." About to give up, the man asks a fourth architect: "What are you drawing?" And that architect finally replies: "I am drawing a cathedral."

I certainly can't predict whether your hand, in the future, will be outfitted with a pencil, a mouse, or a cybernetic glove.

---

8. Fernando Távora, "Pensieri sull'architettura," *Casabella* 678 (2000), 15.

I am not a futurologist, and this of course will not be the main theme of our class. However, as the conclusion of this lecture, I hope that each time in this new millennium that someone asks you what you are drawing, you answer as the fourth architect did. Maybe with the aid of a sketch.

No Day Without a Line: A Lecture on Informed Drawing

1

The "Augmented" Sensitivity of the Architectural Surveyor

I paint what cannot be photographed, and I photograph what I do not wish to paint. If it is a portrait that interests me, a face, or a nude, I will use my camera. It is quicker than making a drawing or a painting. But if it is something I cannot photograph, like a dream or a subconscious impulse, I have to resort to drawing or painting.[1]

Man Ray

I've always been fascinated by the resemblance (and not just phonetic) of "dreaming" and "drawing": two words that, despite having very different etymological roots, describe two activities that have always had a give-and-take, collaborative relationship.

Likewise—despite all the questions raised by the promoters of the "hard sciences"—we constantly forget that the scientist needs poetry, and that the poet can't do without science. The great romantic poet Giacomo Leopardi, for example, when he described the face of the "beautiful moon," knew about Galileo Galilei's astronomic discoveries and was perfectly aware of the fact that what he was anthropomorphizing were in fact valleys and craters. And vice versa: the French doctor Louis Figuier: despite being a famous naturalist published in the most prestigious scientific journals of the time, launched a new type of theatrical genre (he called it "scientific theater") aimed at inspiring the love of science in common people with a variety of short plays about humanity's great inventors.

On the other hand, if it's true that, as Man Ray said, only drawing allows us to express our dreams, it is just as true that

---

1. "Man Ray—Interview in Camera," Paris; reprinted in *Man Ray: photographe*, ed. Philippe Sers (Paris: Centre Georges Pompidou, 1981).

those who cannot dream are not able to draw either. Because only the dreamer-slash-drawer (or, to coin a truly cacophonous neologism, the "dreamdrawer") is able to communicate emotions as well as information, even if sometimes the means are confused with the ends. I'm referring to a slogan coined by the Luxembourgish architect Léon Krier, "I am an architect, because I don't build." It's true that the echo of this provocative sentence has long hovered over the "paper architecture" (projects that were intended only for the drawing board, not to be built) of the postmodern era. Krier's rebuke has debased the beauty of drawings that were too refined, in which the presentation elbowed aside (and in a way obscured) the content of the ideas.

But it's also true that the milestones in architectural history are marked by the explosive force of drawings, drawings that are able to loosen our most secure certainties, going far beyond the banalities of appearance. Think of Giovanni Battista Piranesi with his *Carceri d'invenzione*, fabulous, gloomy etchings of a subterranean jail with huge stone vaults and machinery whose purpose is unclear but which inspire dread in the viewer nonetheless. Another example is Étienne-Louis Boullée, whose "architecture by the light of the moon" has monumental elements dramatized by dramatic alternations of light and shadow. Think too of Yakov Chernikhov: his "architectural fantasies" represented over-the-top constructions that echoed the cinematographic theories of Sergei Eisenstein. These men were all great architects who, despite building little, changed the future of architecture by subverting the way their contemporaries looked at the past.

Identical, too, is the visionary bent that inspires two letters of Vincent van Gogh, in which the destinies of the drawing and the dream are linked by a knot that can't be untied. The first was written to his brother Theo, in which Van Gogh proclaims that "the pencil is the skeleton key that springs the lock and opens the door to the dream." The other letter was to his sister Wilhelmina, in which he proclaims that "the bizarre lines, purposely selected and multiplied, meandering all through the picture, may fail to give the garden a vulgar resemblance, but may present it to our minds as seen in a dream."

These two letters, both written for others (but which have an introspective quality), tell us why any architectural survey can't limit itself to simply recording the material dimensions of the visible city. It has to provide us with the immaterial dimensions of the invisible city as well. (Imagine looking at a survey of Abbey Road in London, but one without the zebra stripes on the cover of the Beatles album of the same name.) Van Gogh's two letters spell out the reasons for which the "augmented" sensitivity of the architectural surveyor is as ancient as humanity itself (and in any event much older than the smartphone).

In that sense, it should not be hard to convince yourselves that an architectural survey has always been and always will be an activity that is *free* (liberated from all rigid, preconceived ideas), *creative* (able to reveal unexpected characteristics of the surrounding world), and *progressive* (ready to replace metric precision with cultural appropriateness). I'm thinking of the mutilated (and gloomy) statues in the notebooks of Carlo Aymonino: out of them comes the premonition that only unfinished pieces, partial fragments, and interrupted vestiges can seep out of the past. I think of the scenes of the film *Amarcord*, where the squares and the porticoes of fascist Rimini were reconstructed on the sets in Rome's Cinecittà, based on the drawings sketched from memory by Federico Fellini during a road trip with his constant companion, Tonino Guerra. They are just sketches, but with a far greater ability to communicate than any computer simulation.

The fact is that we should never reduce drawing to a mere vehicle of iconic proliferation, because, to paraphrase Wittgenstein, it is the driver. Likewise we should never feel at the mercy of technological consumerism, because when we make an "informed survey" (and I'll get to what that means), the only instruments that are indispensable are our heads, our hands, and our hearts. This lecture is also (and above all) dedicated to the making of an architectural survey. This kind of surveying has its roots in the Renaissance and is a particularity of some European architecture, but one that is applicable to our modern era, and not simply here on the old continent. In this lecture I'll make the arguments for its importance to architects everywhere. I'll support my thesis with references from outside of architecture, and with quotes in various languages (though I'll be sure to translate). This text is supposed to be open to everything and everyone, despite the difficulty in the "translation" of the name of a discipline—the architectural survey—which has its roots in Renaissance humanism and, if you look closely, is something that has until now been peculiar to the Italian architectural tradition.

2
The Eyes Are Blind to the Unexpected

I've thought for quite a while about what theme to develop in this first lecture of my Architectural Survey course. I think this course is a golden opportunity for stimulating an intellectual conversation between a teacher and a student, one in which both are on the same wavelength: the kind of conversation that is the basis of any university that merits the name. So today, instead of going through the syllabus and talking about how I grade (something that's necessary, but which we'll get to later), I'd like to make my point of view clear, so we can start out on the same page. First a definition to write down: "architectural survey" means "the mass of operations, of measurement and of analysis, done in order to understand and document an architectural example in all its totality, in its measurable dimensions, in its historical complexity, in its structural and constructive characteristics, in addition to the formal and functional ones."

This is taken from the "Charter of the Architectural Survey," drawn up in Paris in 1999 on the occasion of the international convention "Science et technologie pour la sauvegarde du patrimoine culturel dans les pays du bassin méditerranéen" (Science and Technology for the Safeguarding of the Cultural Heritage in the Countries of the Mediterranean Basin). This definition, despite being quite broad and having been collaboratively written by a pool of the most renowned international experts, doesn't satisfy me, because I find it weighted toward buildings of what is called "historical-artistic patrimony." In other words, important buildings that have lots of documents describing them. Today I'll try to convince you that a factory building deserves the same effort as a paleo-Christian church and that the emotional dimensions are not second to the physical ones.

I'm convinced that architecture's greatest challenge in the coming years will be to be able to imagine a future without throwing away the past, and with it the tradition of attention to unusual points of view. I'm thinking here of the examples of spontaneous architectural solutions, like the suburban inventiveness captured by the artist Dionisio González, and the discovery of the banal everyday, like the evocative rooms of Arduino Cantàfora. They do their work without snobby distinctions between "high culture" and "low culture," but also without making specious distinctions between knowledge and conception. It's not an accident that in my course, I won't build the traditional walls between survey drawing and project design—between drawing something that already exists, and drawing something you want to build—because in my opinion there is a reciprocal solidarity between the two types of drawing.

For this reason it's possible that, now and then, you might feel disoriented, thinking that you're taking a course on Architectural Composition rather than the Architectural Survey. But we'll look at the analytical meticulousness of the tables in which Jean-Nicolas-Louis Durand, in his *Précis des leçons d'architecture*, didn't limit himself to cataloging the repertoire of *éléments simples* but rather tried to classify, experimentally, all their infinite combinations. In the course of this lecture we also won't underestimate the so-called "minor buildings" by limiting our interest to our "historical and artistic patrimony" (i.e., the buildings in tourist guidebooks).

We won't focus on those buildings because I agree with Paul Valéry, who says we should be open to the surprises which only history with a small "h" knows how to produce. As the French historian Fernand Braudel famously said, the grand events of history are "surface disturbances, crests of foam that the tides of history carry on their strong backs." The world in which you will work is dotted with a miniscule number of "signed" works but is full of anonymous buildings. The risks that architectural surveys run in this exceedingly delicate historical moment come from the inadequacies (in both tools and techniques) of a discipline unhinged by a technological revolution that is as dense with historical-ideological encrustations as it is pregnant with expressive potential. What does that mean? I think that architecture is caught between the pencil and Auto-CAD, the Pantheon and housing projects, and it needs to find its way forward.

It's evident that while the survey of "quality" architecture is more or less consolidated (of course there can always be additions, but they are not easily accepted), the survey of architecture "without quality" is still to be written. The reevaluation and rebuilding of the most decrepit parts of our cities demand a review of the fundamentals of architecture, today for some reason neglected. We have to start from the identification of the *genius loci*: the "spirit of the place" because of which, according to Martin Heidegger, the place isn't simply there before the bridge, it is created by the bridge: "The bridge swings over the stream 'with ease and power.' It does not just connect banks that are already there. The banks emerge as banks only as the bridge crosses the stream. The bridge designedly causes them to lie across from each other. One side is set off against the other by the bridge."[2]

Heidegger's example, though referring to a bridge in Heidelberg, seems to me to be particularly pertinent to this introduction because the survey, in its most refined conception, is exactly this. It builds a bridge between the certainties that give you faith in the stability of the "river bank of the past," and the uncertainties that make you wonder about the instability of the "river bank of the future." This gives a certain sense to everything that otherwise would not make sense, unless we abandon the thoroughfares of the known for the paths of the unknown. Just as Pablo Picasso did in painting and Igor Stravinsky in music. Just as Martha Graham in dance when, realizing the beauty of modernity, she put away the tutu and forbade dance *en pointe*, minimizing the presence of costumes and introducing the technique known today as *contraction-release*.

Without this break with the past, postmodern dance would never have existed. Or better, we would have seen neither the performances of *contact improvisation* invented by Steve Paxton (in which the human body is molded by many forms of accidental contact) nor the choreographies created by Dein Perry for *Tap Dogs* (in which the muscular potential of the working classes fuses with the rhythmic agility of tap dancers). I'll get back to architecture, where we see a similar situation: there is a widely shared opinion that, in Europe, the best bet for

2. Martin Heidegger, *Poetry, Language, Thought*, trans. Albert Hofstadter (New York: Harper Perennial Modern Classics, 2001), 150.

the future lies not in the perfection of restoration techniques for the grand buildings of our cities' centers, but rather in finding ways to redeem the decrepit parts of suburban areas.

In shifting from the upkeep of "quality" architecture (Great Buildings) to renovating those "without quality" (housing projects), our cultural baggage and technical instruments for surveys have to be updated and renewed. In the future, we won't simply have lengths to measure, alignments to monitor, and forms to represent. "Precision" will no longer just mean a number exact to the third decimal place; it will be more about concept and less about materials. Above all, more than reducing the iconic superabundance of the architecture of the past, you will work to supply that deficit in the buildings of the present.

Though absolutely necessary (as a quote attributed to Goethe explains, "The eye sees what the mind knows"), all this will be anything but easy. As Karl Popper said, "When faced with the unexpected, our eyes are blind." Ultimately, though, you are in this classroom to prepare yourselves to face tomorrow's challenges with your eyes open. Given that the future of what I will teach you in the next few months is (to put it mildly) uncertain, I want to embolden you. I'll do this by telling you about the sacred origins of the architectural survey, which are not always given adequate attention. I'll do this by reciting a biblical passage in which the priest Ezekiel is seized with a vision of an angel sent by God to give him the measurements (and with them, the characteristics) of a new stone temple destined to replace the precariousness of the Tabernacle (Ezekiel 40:1–49). It's a passage that (as is well known) is the prelude to the New Jerusalem, and which (much less noted) constitutes the first example of a literary description of an architectural survey.

In the twenty-fifth year of our exile, at the beginning of the year, on the tenth day of the month, in the fourteenth year after the city was conquered, on that very day, the hand of the LORD was upon me, and brought me in the visions of God into the land of Israel, and set me down upon a very high mountain, on which was a structure like a city opposite me. When he brought me there, behold, there was a man, whose appearance was like bronze, with a line of flax and a measuring reed in his hand; and he was standing in the gateway. And the man said to me, "Son of man, look with your eyes, and hear with your ears, and set your mind upon all that I shall show you, for you were brought here in order that I might show it to you; declare all that you see to the house of Israel.

And behold, there was a wall all around the outside of the temple area, and the length of the measuring reed in the man's hand was six long cubits, each being a cubit and a handbreadth in length; so he measured the thickness of the wall, one reed; and the height, one reed. Then he went into the gateway facing east, going up its steps, and measured the threshold of the gate, one reed deep; and the side rooms, one reed long, and one reed broad; and the space between the side rooms, five cubits; and the threshold of the gate by the vestibule of the gate at the inner end, one reed. Then he measured the vestibule of the gateway, eight cubits; and its jambs, two cubits; and the vestibule of the gate was at the inner end. And there were three side rooms on either side of the east gate; the three were of the same size; and the jambs on either side were of the same size. Then he measured the breadth of the opening of the gateway, ten cubits; and the breadth of the gateway, thirteen cubits. There was a barrier before the side rooms, one cubit on either side; and the side rooms were six cubits on either side. Then he measured the gate from the back of the one side room to the back of the other, a breadth of five and twenty cubits, from door to door. He measured also the vestibule, twenty cubits; and round about the vestibule of the gateway was the court. From the front of the gate at the entrance to the end of the inner vestibule of the gate was fifty cubits. And the gateway had windows round about, narrowing inwards into their jambs in the side rooms, and likewise the vestibule had windows round about inside, and on the jambs were palm trees.

Then he brought me into the outer court; and behold, there were chambers and a pavement, round about the court; thirty chambers fronted on the pavement. And the pavement ran along the side of the gates, corresponding to the length of the gates; this was the lower pavement. Then he measured the distance from the inner front of the lower gate to the outer front of the inner court, a hundred cubits.

Then he went before me to the north, and behold, there was a gate which faced toward the north, belonging to the outer court. He measured its length and its breadth. Its side rooms, three on either side, and its jambs and its vestibule were of the same size as those of the first gate; its length was fifty cubits, and its breadth twenty-five cubits. And its windows, its vestibule, and its palm trees were of the same size as those of the gate which faced toward the east; and seven steps led up to it; and its vestibule was on the inside. And opposite the gate on the north, as on the east, was a gate to the inner court; and he measured from gate to gate, a hundred cubits. And he led me toward the south, and behold, there was a gate on the south; and he measured its jambs and its vestibule; they had the same size as the others. And there were windows round about in it and in its vestibule, like the windows of the others; its length was fifty cubits, and its breadth twenty-five cubits. And there were seven steps leading up to it, and its vestibule was on the inside; and it had palm trees on its jambs, one on either side. And there was a gate on the south of the inner court; and he measured from gate to gate toward the south, a hundred cubits.

Then he brought me to the inner court by the south gate, and he measured the south gate; it was of the same size as the others. Its side rooms, its jambs, and its vestibule were of the same size as the others; and there were windows round about in it and in its vestibule; its length was fifty cubits, and its breadth twenty-five cubits. And there were vestibules round about, twenty-five cubits long and five cubits broad. Its vestibule faced the outer court, and palm trees were on its jambs, and its stairway had eight steps. Then he brought me to the inner court on the east side, and he measured the gate; it was of the same size as the others. Its side rooms, its jambs, and its vestibule were of the same size as the others; and there were windows round about in it and in its vestibule; its length was fifty cubits, and its breadth twenty-five cubits. Its vestibule faced the outer court, and it had palm trees on its jambs, one on either side; and its stairway had eight steps.

Then he brought me to the north gate, and he measured it; it had the same size as the others. Its side rooms, its jambs, and its vestibule were of the same size as the others; and it had windows round about; its length was fifty cubits, and its breadth twenty-five cubits. Its vestibule faced the outer court, and it had palm trees on its jambs, one on either side; and its stairway had eight steps. There was a chamber with its door in the vestibule of the gate, where the burnt offering was to be washed. And in the vestibule of the gate were two tables on either side, on which the burnt offering and the sin offering and the guilt offering were to be slaughtered. And on the outside of the vestibule at the entrance of the north gate were two tables; and on the other side of the vestibule of the gate were two tables. Four tables were on the inside, and four tables on the outside of the side of the gate, eight tables, on which the sacrifices were to be slaughtered. And there were also four tables of hewn stone for the burnt offering, a cubit and a half long, and a cubit and a half broad, and one cubit high, on which the instruments were to be laid with which the burnt offerings and the sacrifices were slaughtered. And hooks, a handbreadth long, were fastened round about within. And on the tables the flesh of the offering was to be laid.

Then he brought me from without into the inner court, and behold, there were two chambers in the inner court, one at the side of the north gate facing south, the other at the side of the south gate facing north. And he said to me, This chamber which faces south is for the priests who have charge of the temple, and the chamber which faces north is for the priests who have charge of the altar; these are the sons of Zadok, who alone among the sons of Levi may come near to the LORD to minister to him. And he measured the court, a hundred cubits long, and a hundred cubits broad, foursquare; and the altar was in front of the temple.

Then he brought me to the vestibule of the temple and measured the jambs of the vestibule, five cubits on either side; and the breadth of the gate was fourteen cubits; and the sidewalls of the gate were three cubits on either side. The length of the vestibule was twenty cubits, and the breadth twelve cubits; and ten steps led up to it; and there were pillars beside the jambs on either side. (Revised Standard Version)

Despite risking putting you to sleep (the repetitive style of the Torah has that effect), I wanted to read you that whole text for two reasons. The first is a general reason: as the philosopher Massimo Cacciari says, our "forma mentis" (the form of the mind) in the West has its roots in the Bible. That book, demanding interpretations and asking questions, has made us constantly transform how we look at the tradition, and occasionally revolutionized our understanding of it. The second reason is specific: Ezekiel's vision is the perfect pretext for claiming the indispensability of drawing for thinking. We see here that drawing wasn't born as an instrument to presage what's to come, but as a tool to remember.

Here we can see a vestige of drawing's mythological origins. One story about the birth of drawing has been handed down to us by the ancient Roman writer Pliny the Elder, in his work *Natural History*. According to Pliny, a young maiden from Sicyon, to capture the memory of her beloved before his departure on a long journey, traced the shadow of his face in profile. Another version—this time a medieval one recounted by Petrarch in his *On Illustrious Men*—tells of Ninus (the king of the Assyrians) who, when his father Belus died, had a portrait made of him, to be worshipped by Ninus's subjects. Did you know that Nicholas of Lyra and Isaac Newton both attempted, in vain, to reconstruct the plan of the temple as described by Ezekiel? The impossibility of "graphic translation" (in other words, re-creation) of the "survey" set out by the biblical angel shows us that it's impossible to rebuild buildings described only by literary texts.

This makes me think of the inevitable differences in artistic representations of hell as described by Dante Alighieri in his *Divine Comedy*: they run from the unsettling watercolors of William Blake, to Gustave Doré's vibrant etchings, to the cold miniatures of Attilio Razzolini. It would also be impossible to reconstruct the languid rococo atmosphere that hovers over the Parisian *maison de plaisance* traced out by Jean-François de Bastide in *La petite maison* (The Little House: An Architectural Seduction), where we follow the courting of the beautiful Mélite by the cunning Marquis de Trémicour. On the other hand, we can see the influence of Marguerite Yourcenar's novel *Denier du rêve* on an entire generation of neorealist cinematographers. In this book the daily rituals of the protagonist's group of friends overlap in a Rome that oscillates between "super-city" (caught by the onset of unscrupulous real estate speculation) and "super-village" (populated by women with hair curlers and dressing gowns who distractedly water the flowers crammed onto their balconies).

It's not a coincidence that when Leonardo da Vinci realized he could capture his scientific observations better in drawing than with words, he stated this clearly in his anatomical notebook. This makes me think of the legend according to which Robert Louis Stevenson was inspired to write *Treasure Island* by a drawing. The story, curious to say the least, has it that Stevenson was vacationing in the Scottish Highland village of Braemar with his family, including his stepson Lloyd Osbourne. Lloyd was absorbed with making a watercolor of a map of an island and Stevenson was so struck by it that he began to name all the imaginary places on the map, and labeled it, in one of the map's corners, "Treasure Island." It was his stepson who supposedly said something like, "What fun it would be to read a story about this treasure island!"

Stevenson, at the time just thirty years old, got right to work. He wrote the first fifteen chapters one right after another and published them serially in the magazine *Young Folks*. The success was such that, in just a few years, the adventures of Jim Hawkins became a bestseller for young people everywhere. They still are today. Interestingly enough, when the publisher decided to publish the famous map that had inspired it all at the back of a new edition of the book, Stevenson not only couldn't find it, he couldn't even remember what it had looked like. To redraw that now-famous map, he had to reread his own book line by line. The moral is simple: *rêverie* and survey (or rather, "fantastical narration" and "evocative drawing") are two distinct activities which overlap only when they move from the technical realm to the poetic one. This is obvious in a story of the great illustrator and draftsman Gaspare De Fiore. At the end of a memorable duet-duel with the great graphic artist Alfred Hohenegger, De Fiore charmed the audience (and the jury) with his recounting of an experience that he had had in the monastery of the Trinity Lavra of St. Sergius, where the tomb of St. Sergius is. I'll cite De Fiore's words exactly as they are in the transcript:

> In this monastery, before visiting the saint's tomb, it's customary
> to confer with the [Russian Orthodox] Pope to reveal to him
> one's prayer. The Pope then writes the prayer in Cyrillic letters on

a slip of paper and gives it to the faithful person. Because I didn't know how to speak or write in Russian, I "surveyed" my soul and drew an angel to express my desire to say a prayer to my guardian angel. The Pope looked at my drawing, folded the paper, and gave it back to me. In front of the tomb there's a brazier where the prayer slips are burnt. Ahead of me a Russian peasant woman, who had just received a prayer written out by the Pope, put hers in the fire. It burned and the smoke rose up to heaven. After her, I put my slip in the brazier, and my illustrated prayer, just like the written one before it, burned and rose up to heaven.[3]

This suggests the difficulty of defining the architectural survey (or in the Romance languages, the "relief") in the era of the 3D scanner and GPS. This is obvious from debates about the history of the word "relief." In my opinion the best hypothesis for its etymology has been put forward by Roberto Masiero. Like everyone else he starts with the Latin verb *relaevo*, but he digs further, back down to its most archaic form: *laevo*. This word, considered by itself, means "to render smooth," while the Latin prefix *re-* indicates an inversion, a "going against." In this sense something that has been surveyed (with an architectural *relief*) is something that, from smooth and indistinct, becomes emergent and more distinct, in that *relaevo* means "to lift, to raise." Three things are necessary: someone who carries out the action of raising (the surveyor), something that must and can be raised (the object of the survey or relief), and—most importantly—a surface with respect to which the action of raising has meaning (the superficial appearance of the object of the survey).

---

3. Paolo Belardi and Valeria Menchetelli, eds., *Duetto: disegnare per dire, scrivere per dire* (Perugia: Università degli Studi di Perugia, 2006), 41–42.

Thus the word "relief" seems quite elusive. At this point the only way to understand what it means is to draw continuously (like the precept *Nulla dies sine linea*, "No day without a line [drawn]," attributed to the Greek painter Apelles) and to think discontinuously (exactly as the era of the text message and social networks would have us do). But remember that the architectural survey is never a zero-sum game, because one thing is sure: after having done it, we know more than we did before. Therefore, today I'll put off starting our drawing exercises and I'll lay out my thesis in three parts (perhaps a bit all over the place, but certainly synergistic). Each is dedicated to one of three themes. These correspond to three dimensions of informed survey drawing which, in my opinion, best describe the distance between technical drawing and humanistic drawing: x (width/exploration), y (height/stratification), and z (depth/interpretation). I'll do this adopting the spatial dimensions of projective geometry, where the xy plane coincides with the projective plane. At the end of the day, the reference points of a surveyor are still the ones Renaissance artists called "perspectiva artificialis."

3
X_width/exploration

Until now the architectural survey has had two contradictory approaches: on one hand, taking objective measurements and turning them into images on paper; on the other, selecting information for specific purposes and presenting descriptions of the characteristics important for those purposes. I want to tell you that you should not—and won't have to—split your-selves between these two roles. One is that of the impartial compiler who collects data and leaves it to others to do the critical analysis, the other that of the partial interpreter who independently formulates hypotheses, sometimes even shoe-horning them into reality. You won't have to split yourselves in the sense that, if you want to, you can take a third approach whose position on the x axis is both between and quite far away from the other two approaches: perhaps at infinity. This ap-proach is aimed at practicing architectural surveying together with deepening knowledge, an approach we could call that of the surveyor-detective.

This is someone who will have to face jigsaw puzzles that are missing most of their pieces (it's not a coincidence that jig-saw puzzles were invented by the cartographer John Spilsbury). It's someone who will have to find and compare relics of the past—hopefully without running the risks that Indiana Jones did. It's someone who will frequent musty storerooms and for-gotten archives where, in addition to letters and technical draw-ings, he or she can study those construction site documents that few researchers pay attention to: professional reports, bid con-tracts, estimated computations, and official tests. It's someone who will combine the descriptive ability of a semiotician with the prescriptive ability of a doctor; the future of architecture in general, and in particular of the architectural survey, lies in the integration of all these tasks.

It's someone whose gaze will not only be directed back-ward but also forward, because he or she will be called upon to generate connections between elements that to most people seem unrelated. I don't want to seem naïve: I'm aware that the academic world will look at the figure I've just traced out with diffidence, dismissing it as amateurish. This is a shame, because it's precisely because of this kind of investigative approach that the interdisciplinary team led by Maurizio Seracini, using reflectographic and video-endoscopic techniques, solved the age-old question of the artistic paternity of the *Città ideale* of Urbino (attributed, once and for all, to Leon Battista Alberti). The same team of surveyor-detectives later breathed new life into the theory according to which Leonardo da Vinci's *Battaglia di Anghiari* is hidden in plain sight. They showed that the fresco is located right under the east wall of the Salon of the Five Hundred in the Palazzo Vecchio in Florence, behind a cavity wall only a few centimeters thick, covered by the *Battaglia di Marciano* by Giorgio Vasari.

I'm aware, though, that the figure of the surveyor-detective is particularly important for a society like the present one, a society that is more interested in the immediacy of the scoop or the sensational story than the thorough article. Be careful, because chasing a scoop is risky business: pushing the envelope with hasty hypotheses, if not unwise in itself, could lead to unpleasant consequences. Hopefully they would be less fatal that those suffered by the protagonist of the intrigue narrated in the film *The Draughtsman's Contract*, written and directed by Peter Greenaway in 1982.

The story, which takes place at the end of a late-seventeenth-century summer in the luxurious setting of a delightful villa in the English countryside, begins with the hiring by

Mrs. Herbert (wife of a rich landowner) of one Mr. Neville, a popular landscape draftsman. His contract calls for him to execute twelve drawings of the sumptuous residence, to be given as a sign of reconciliation to Mrs. Herbert's husband, who is away on a brief business trip. Puffed up with his unusual role as a virtual autocrat, Mr. Neville arrogantly imposes his rules on the local community: while he is intently drawing, everyone must move out of the way, removing from his vision any human being. But it is precisely that haughtiness that betrays him.

Disturbing clues begin to appear in this bucolic scene— a ripped shirt, a pair of riding boots, a vest with a tear at the level of the heart, and a spooked horse—which all lead back to Mr. Herbert, making us suspect his murder. The only one who doesn't seem to notice is Mr. Neville himself. Distracted by his obsession with reproducing reality with maniacal care, he unknowingly documents the evidence of the murder; in doing so, he signs his own death warrant. Indeed, when Mr. Herbert's cadaver is found in a garden canal, Mr. Neville (who is now an inconvenient witness) is done away with and his drawings (proof of the crime) are burned.

This suggests that it's not a good idea "to draw what one sees but not what one knows," if for no other reason than because, as always in the architectural survey, the desire to represent clashes with the incomprehensibility of reality. What do I mean by that? Greenaway's cinematographic paradox shows that there are many similarities between the act of investigation and that of the survey. Faced with a mystery, both proceed from the chaos of the unknown toward the order of knowledge; both search for rules and proof in order to give credence to their intuitions; both support, with continual rethinking, the connection between the premises derived from the clues and the conclusions of sound judgment. Who wouldn't agree that the qualities necessary for the surveyor are the same ones that Sherlock Holmes attributes to a detective: the ability to observe, logical reasoning, and knowledge?

It's even more difficult, both for the detective and for the surveyor, to take a step back from the external world, continuously reviewing one's convictions on the basis of the logical concatenation of the data gleaned while on the scene. Not coincidentally, for Sherlock Holmes the decisive moment of investigating was not in deduction or induction but rather abduction. This is a process of formulating explanatory hypotheses open to the fortuitous contribution of serendipity: in other words, a guess about what the explanation is, but one open to the happy revision of chance discoveries. Whereas deduction (which goes from the general to the specific) demonstrates that *something must be* and induction (which goes from the specific to the general) shows that *something really is*, abduction (which formulates a causal hypothesis starting from a perceived effect) suggests that *something could be and that, ultimately, it probably is.*

Holmes is quite explicit about this. In a famous passage from *A Study in Scarlet*, for example, he explains to Dr. Watson that the secret to the solution of the problems of police investigation is in getting back to the beginnings: "In the every-day affairs of life it is more useful to reason forwards, and so the other comes to be neglected.... Most people, if you describe a train of events to them, will tell you what the result would be...."

There are few people, however, who, if you told them a result, would be able to evolve from their own inner consciousness what the steps were which led up to that result."[4]

Holmes doesn't miss the chance to highlight the importance of evidence and clues, giving much importance to negative evidence as well. Think of when Sir Arthur Conan Doyle's detective, while searching for a missing racehorse, is asked by Inspector Gregson, "Is there any point to which you would wish to draw my attention?" Holmes, without missing a beat, responds, "To the curious incident of the dog in the night-time." In a huff, Gregson replies, "The dog did nothing in the night-time." "That was the curious incident," finishes Holmes laconically.[5] Beyond the undeniable affinities between detection and architectural surveying, it's clear that history is not always a technical problem, one whose solution can always be sought as one searches for a person guilty of a crime. But sometimes it is indeed like that. When I was surveying the important monuments of my hometown (Gubbio, in central Italy), I remembered the advice of the great archaeologist Andrea Carandini, according to whom "fantasy is indispensable to the historian: empty critique, empty narration, a concept without intuition are completely sterile."[6] I gave up the role of the Grand Tourist (who uses red chalk to sketch the most picturesque angles of the city) and tried another approach. It's one that is both detached and imaginative, based on an idea of Xavier de Maistre.

4. Arthur Conan Doyle, *A Study in Scarlet*, in *The Complete Sherlock Holmes*, vol. 1 (Garden City, NY: Doubleday, 1930), 83–84.

5. Arthur Conan Doyle, "Silver Blaze," in *The Complete Sherlock Holmes*, 1:347.

6. Andrea Carandini, "E l'archeologo scoprì la fiction," *Corriere della Sera*, 9 April 2010, 47.

His semiautobiographical story "Voyage around My Room" tells how an official under house arrest contemplates each part of his own room as if he were on a voyage. It's a parody of the travel narratives written by the Grand Tourists who traveled by carriage all over Italy, but I used it to see my own city with new eyes, without preconceptions. With these new eyes I began to look at documents that were already well known, but I saw them in a whole new way.

This approach worked, as I revealed the hidden plan that sets out the polyhedral form of the three wooden *ceri* for which Gubbio is famous.[7] Like Holmes, I showed that the man responsible for the project was none other than the painter Fra Carnevale. I also uncovered the surprising geometric similarities between the structure of the church of San Carlo alle Quattro Fontane in Rome and that of the Madonna del Prato in Gubbio, and I was able to reveal the direct involvement of Francesco Borromini in the latter as well. Later I led the same sort of investigation in Perugia, my adopted city. I put together a number of clues to show that the chromosomes of the city's most illustrious institution (the Academy of Fine Arts) have the DNA of Galeazzo Alessi. Alessi was born in Perugia and was one of the greatest Italian architects of the latter half of the sixteenth century. He designed (among other things) the Via Nuova in Genoa and the Palazzo Marino in Milan.

---

7. The *ceri* are three wooden constructions, crowned by the three patron saints of Gubbio (St. Ubaldo, St. George, and St. Anthony the Abbot). They are elaborate geometrical barrels and are a central part of a popular festival that has taken place for more than eight centuries; it takes place on 15 May and celebrates the principal patron saint of Gubbio, St. Ubaldo (c. 1084–1160).

I was able to demonstrate Alessi's involvement thanks to an analysis of a faded manuscript, a chronicle compiled by the painter and mathematician Raffaello Sozi, in which the founding of the Academy was noted as the first event worthy of recording in 1573. The manuscript in question is entitled *Annals, Memories, and Remembrances Beginning in the Year 1540* and is in Perugia's main library. It was well known to scholars and had been published many times, but, rereading it with an investigative approach (that of the surveyor-detective), we can tease out some precious information.

A virtuous multitude of painters and architects had more than once said that it would be full of merit and useful that in the city of Perugia there should be a place where men could come at certain times to discourse on the excellence of drawing, in order that they might more easily come into an understanding of Painting, Sculpture, Architecture, Perspective, Fortifications, and all the other things that Drawing has in its train.

And, considering that the knowledge of the art of Drawing would be of much profit to many in this our city in order to learn the trade of war, where many of us by natural inclination often find ourselves, and likewise that it would be useful to Architecture, which is so full of benefit to noble and magnificent cities, they resolved to publicize this noble and beautiful thought to certain gentlemen, captains and honored citizens of our homeland, who had desire of virtuous things. With infinite pleasure they listened to the proposal, as useful as it was honored, concerning the noble arts of drawing, and they not only consented and approved that frequent encounters to reason about drawing would be of the highest honor to the homeland, but also asked the teachers of Painting, Sculpture, and Architecture that, to the greater glory of the homeland and to the profit of those who desired to exercise themselves in the most noble study of drawing, they should soon initiate an Academy, which having as its principal object virtue, one could certainly hope that in the passage of time it would succeed in producing men excellent and rare.

And having concluded that they should bring forward this laudable proposal, they elected six men to bring about the project's conclusion, and three were of the artists and three of the other number, who immediately elected as protector the most illustrious and most reverend Cardinal of Perugia and humbly beseeched his license as our Bishop to be able to form this assembly; and thereafter asking Monsignor San Felice to be their Governor, he not only consented but asked that they number him among the members of the Academy. And inflamed by the eager exhortation of these principles, their honest and virtuous desires found God's favor, so that they were granted the use of the Chapel of Sant'Angelo della Pace on the hill, built on the basis of the canonical principles of architecture, and recognizing this as a singular grace, they chose as their heavenly patron St. Michael Archangel.

And they began to meet each Sunday and made Orazio Alfani, a superb painter, and Raffaello Sozi the heads of the new Academy of Drawing for the first six months of the year 1573. With much diligence these had the laws of the Academy settled and arranged who would give lectures on Architecture, on Mathematics, and above all had the members do drawing exercises and make statues in clay; they drew many plans of diverse constructions and whoever felt so inclined displayed his work, and in addition they continuously had many learned discourses about diverse things that one does with drawing and its various parts.

And Monsignor Giovanni Tomaso San Felice, our most laudable Governor, having said many times that he wanted one day to come to the Academy to hear a lecture in order to be present at some of the discussions, he was invited one Sunday which was the 27th of June of the said year, giving the members of the Academy to believe that just the Governor would be at the lecture; but the thing played out in another way, as Monsignor the Governor was accompanied by all his chiefs and by many gentlemen and citizens.

And though the lecture had been prepared by Raffaello Sozi privately, it was nonetheless heard publicly, as with much gratitude for almost an hour he discoursed about proportions and the great utility that one receives from them, distinguishing the various types, and applying the understanding of proportions to Painting, Sculpture, and Architecture.

Which having been furnished, Monsignor the Governor with much theory reviewed the principal points of the lecture, and for quite a while, with that singular grace and sweetness with which His Most Reverend Personage customarily does each thing with great prudence, he inflamed the breasts of the new members of the Academy to begin the study of proportions, in order that they might be able to learn the whole art of drawing, and, like one who wisely had acquired a name in all the various parts of drawing, he reasoned in the form of a lecture on many beautiful and learned inventions in painting and sculpture. This done, unanimously the members thanked him from their hearts for the great favor that he had deigned to show them, and they accompanied him to the palace.[8]

As other scholars from various disciplines have already noted, Sozi's text gives us striking insights into the relationship between the new academic institution and Perugian cultural life in that era: the initiative to found an institution that was academic and included artists ("a virtuous multitude of painters

_____
8. Raffaello Sozi, "Principio della Academia del Dissegno," in *Annali, memorie, et ricordi, scritte da Rafaello Sotij cominciando l'anno MDXL*, Perugia, second half of the sixteenth century, p. 115 (Biblioteca Comunale Augusta di Perugia, ms. 1221).

and architects"), academic life energized by theoretical debate ("to discourse on the excellence of drawing"), and the academic structure founded on the centrality of drawing ("that they might more easily come into an understanding of Painting, Sculpture, Architecture, Perspective, Fortifications").

As I've already mentioned, in my opinion this shows the ideological paternity of Galeazzo Alessi—a paternity which until then had been supported only by a rather weak piece of evidence, the brief interval between Alessi's death (30 December 1572) and the foundation of the "Academy of Drawing" (the first months of 1573). With a closer reading of the document, we can pick out and put together the clues sown by Sozi throughout his chronicle.

First clue. From the *Annals* we can see that the first members of the Academy "elected as protector the most illustrious and most reverend Cardinal of Perugia," Fulvio Della Corgna, and "beseeched his license as our Bishop to be able to form this assembly." Fulvio Della Corgna was linked to Alessi not only by a personal bond of trust which led him to give Alessi prestigious offices (including, in 1572, that of councillor of Perugia) but also professionally, which led him to appoint Alessi to other duties (among others, in 1568, the design of the main portal of Perugia's cathedral).

Second clue. From the *Annals* we can see that initially the Academy was "granted the use of the Chapel of Sant'Angelo della Pace on the hill." This church in the Porta Sole neighborhood of Perugia, despite its small dimensions, represented the most significant work left by Alessi to his native city. It is an excellent example of the habit, typical of Alessi, of "building on the built" and sealing each change of urban space with theatrical microarchitecture.

Third clue. From the *Annals* again we read that on "the 27th of June of the said year" (1573) there was an actual inauguration ceremony, ending with a lecture given by Sozi himself, who "with much gratitude for almost an hour ... discoursed about proportions and the great utility that one receives from them." It's a theme that is not foreign to the local cultural context, as it is central to the speculative theories advanced by the erudite Perugians of the age (from Giovan Battista Caporali to Vincenzo and Egnazio Danti). Alessi himself, in the preface to his book *Libro dei misteri*, specifies that the small chapels in his new plan of the Sacred Mountain of Varallo are rendered beautiful by the correctness of their geometric proportions, or in his words "with all the order and décor of architecture."

At the risk of repetition, it's important for me to repeat to you that when you do historical research (all the more if that research is part of an architectural survey), you have to go beyond the written and oral sources. The "material sources"— what you actually see in front of you—have to be taken into consideration, especially if they lead to a slew of unanswered questions. This is because, to borrow the phrase that inspector Jules Maigret used to seal the success of his investigations, the most important questions are those to which no response can be given. It's this famous attention of Maigret to both the interior life and the exterior behavior of his suspects that makes me think of one last recommendation: if you take the approach of the surveyor-detective, avoid confusing the means with the end. By this I mean don't put too much faith (or at least don't trust blindly) in technology.

This has been amply demonstrated by the failure of a number of recent investigations conducted by the Italian magistrates into confusing murders. In these investigations, the police (having renounced any kind of direct investigation) placed their trust blindly in forensic evidence-gathering done by the "Scientific Investigation Department" of the national police in Parma. But the resulting impasse of the investigations confirms that—to paraphrase the insightful observation of the French astrophysicist Jean-Pierre Luminet—the mysteries of history (like those of life) are resolved less by use of a microscope (or telescope) than by imagination.

4

Y_height/stratification

I'll begin discussing architectural stratification using as a talking point an excerpt full of pathos from the journal of Heinrich Schliemann, in which he describes all of the phases of a decisive dig in Aeolis. Aeolis is a region in Turkey between the Hellespont in the north and the mouth of the Gediz River in the south, known to the world as the place where the ancient Greek poet Homer was born. The journal describes in detail how Schliemann found, as he dug, one epoch's city, then another, earlier city, then yet another. When they reached virgin soil, they had found four layers of city walls as well as three other prehistoric settlements.

Schliemann's words leave no room for doubt that ancient Pergamon, like every other ancient city all across the world, grew on top of itself. This fact, however—and here we get right into our discussion—should not compromise our ability to imagine the incredible theatrical effect of the "great marble altar, forty feet high, with impressive statues, and entirely surrounded by a battle of giants." These are the words of Lucius Ampelius, referring to the monument raised by Eumenes II to celebrate his victory over the Galatians, today rebuilt in the Pergamon-museum in Berlin. It also cannot hinder us from appreciating the forms shaped by that extraordinary architect that Franco Purini has christened "the Time Factor": an anonymous architect, but with a capital "A," that has left us not only mounds of ruins (like Pergamon) as an inheritance, but also the streets and squares of our historic city centers, putting its mark, stratum upon stratum, on the axes of the grid.

I'll attempt to explain myself better with an example. If you stood at the hilltop panoramic point in the Carducci Gardens in Perugia, an archaeologist could provide you with a fantastic plan, a stratigraphic (layer-by-layer) reconstruction on paper of the area you're looking down at. She might have indicated the positions of the medieval housing blocks in red, for example, the cordon of the fourteenth-century city walls in yellow, and the routes of the nineteenth-century street rebuilding in blue. At first glance, this diagram would seem divorced from what you have before your eyes. This despite the fact that, through a process of mental acceleration, you could attempt a similar visual peeling away and architectural decoding. But if you look up from this technical document and forget all its centuries, if you put aside any vain desire to X-ray your surroundings, you'll be charmed by the uniqueness of this incredible urban reality. Here the submerged and the surface city live together without obvious discontinuity.

Even if it's true that the Italian historic city centers are occasionally the fruit of some unified vision (I'm thinking here of the Addizione Erculea in Ferrara), much more frequently they are made from houses built below an aqueduct (like the Bourbon aqueduct in Atrani), from defensive ramparts converted into covered streets (like the Via degli Asini in Brisighella), or from amphitheaters transformed into palaces (like the Cancello neighborhood in Formia). In other words, we can see not only results that were planned, but also unplanned outcomes that we *perceive* as intentional. I'll try to resolve the inherent ambiguity with a concrete example. If we find ourselves in front of the church at the abbey of San Galgano, near Siena, we're struck by the lack of a roof, but we don't try to mentally reconstruct the original space. On the contrary, what excites us is precisely the uniqueness of the ruined state, with the grassy pavement and the beams of sunlight that filter though the tall, mullioned window of the nave.

It's the same with the Renaissance loggia of the church of the Twelve Holy Apostles in Rome, where the contrast between the dynamism of the first order of columns and the rigor of the attachment to the ground is determined by the baroque alterations to the original structure. These were done when (following the plan of Carlo Rainaldi) the space between the upper columns was walled up, partially perforated with wide decorated windows, and then crowned with a totally new balustrade.

It doesn't matter to us anymore that in both cases the present configurations were determined by events that were absolutely independent of the original architectural plan. In the case of the abbey, the dismantling of the roof was caused by the negligence of the commissioning abbot Girolamo Vitelli. In the Roman basilica, the functional restoration was ordered by Cardinal Brancati di Lauria. Stop writing and listen as I repeat that point: what we perceive, copy in our sketchbooks, and memorize are the *final* architectural forms in front of our eyes. These forms, however, are not the result of processes of architectural *addition* only, but also of *subtraction.*

Indeed, if the church of the Twelve Holy Apostles is like layers of sedimentation, betraying the progressive "decomposition" of the original plan, the abbey of San Galgano finds its expressive power in its present condition of a ruin. The ruin is perhaps the most dramatic form of dismantling: the unity of the initial building is negated by the structural decomposition and, with it, the progressive reabsorption into the natural landscape. It's an extreme condition but a privileged one, as it's the only one that bares to view, with dramatic completeness, the poetic nature of architecture. Francesco Venezia said it best:

> We continue to appreciate in ruins, even if in disrepair, a venerable set of relationships. Despite the fact that the missing parts affect the music's completeness and harmony, we perceive the pathetic condition that renders the building almost part of nature, almost geography. Another reaction acts upon our sensibility: as humans, we are proud to have created something that has almost returned to nature.[9]

9. Francesco Venezia, *La natura poetica dell'architettura, The poetic nature of architecture* (Pordenone: Giavedoni Editore, 2010), 16.

The fact is that, willing or not, we are beguiled by the organic lives of buildings. Despite being inanimate, they are like living beings. They prefer to survive, accepting the need to adapt to the changing needs of each age, rather than disappear because of a vain refusal to change.

When we recognize how stratified architecture involves a degree of complexity and individuality not equally possible in a building that was conceived and executed as a whole, it changes how we feel about architecture. We feel the weight of superimposed thoughts, and we ourselves become involved in those examples in which innovation appears so totally in debt to the preexisting situation that it seems almost gratuitous. We can see the same motivations in a passage from Nathaniel Hawthorne's novel *The Marble Faun*; they drive a group of Anglo-American artists doing the classic moonlight stroll to leave the direct route from Trajan's Forum to the Coliseum, in order to see "the effort of Time to bury up the ancient city, as if it were a corpse, and he the sexton."

> The party moved on, but deviated a little from the straight way, in order to glance at the ponderous remains of the temple of Mars Ultor, within which a convent of nuns is now established—a dovecote, in the war god's mansion. At only a little distance, they passed the portico of a Temple of Minerva, most rich and beautiful in architecture, but woefully gnawed by time and shattered by violence, besides being buried midway in the accumulation of soil, that rises over dead Rome like a flood tide. Within this edifice of antique sanctity, a baker's shop was now established, with an entrance on one side; for, everywhere, the remnants of old grandeur and divinity have been made available for the meanest necessities of today.[10]

10. Nathaniel Hawthorne, *The Marble Faun* (New York: Houghton Mifflin, 1860), vol. 1, 168.

Hawthorne's words evoke the structuralist concept of the palimpsest. This term originally referred to a piece of parchment whose text had been mostly wiped away so the piece could be reused for another document, but where faded vestiges remained under the new text. When we look at the architectural equivalents of the palimpsest, we can see all the contradictions that were not planned in the original architectural design. These are things that an architectural survey must consider, if for no other reason than that (to cite the shrewd saying of Wim Wenders) the scars of a city hide centuries of history. Or perhaps it would be better to say that they *reveal* centuries of history, giving architecture an aura of mystery.

And with it, some ambiguity. For example, in Palazzo Tarugi in Montepulciano: does the corner, involuntarily accentuated by the obstruction of the loggia above it, take priority over the centrality of the whole as conceived by Antonio da Sangallo the Elder? What about the basilica of San Venanzio in Camerino: is the sense of being out of scale caused by the minute order of the bas-reliefs that decorate the fourteenth-century portal, or the neoclassical pronaos's gigantic order of columns added by Luigi Poletti? At the same time, we feel a sort of irrelevance when confronted with architectural constructions that have remained unchanged during the course of the centuries. Their seeming "completeness" makes us suspicious and gives them the feel of an archaeological dig or a museum rather than a city. Think of the monotonous unity of entire city centers frozen in time, like Carcassonne, Toledo, or the upper city in Bergamo.

We all know that any kind of architecture, to become part of the urban fabric, must evolve as a "dialectical building." I mean that it has to take on a significant role in the urban geography of a city not merely because of its permanence on a map, but also because of its successive modifications. We can see one of the most elementary forms of stratification—incorporation into another building—in the basilica of Santa Maria degli Angeli in Assisi, where Galeazzo Alessi incorporated the tiny church called the Porziuncola (rebuilt by St. Francis) into the basilica. The same is true of the Ara Pacis Museum in Rome, which Richard Meier built around the Augustan monument. The idea remains the same, because the ability to measure the immaterial dimensions of architecture depends on who does the measuring, not on the building measured.

This is true above all if the temporal dimension is involved, because the perception of the passing of time (which is definitely a form of surveying) is by definition subjective. Albert Einstein was clear about this. When he wanted to explain with simple words the theory of relativity, he supposedly gave a very concrete example: "When a man sits with a pretty girl for an hour, it seems like a minute. But let him sit on a hot stove for a minute and it's longer than any hour. That's relativity."[11] I'm sure you will all agree that the man can't perceive how much time has passed in the two situations in the same way.

This is the reason for the eternal clash between "scientific time" (objectively measurable through the various instruments used throughout the centuries, from the hourglass to the mechanical watch to digital chronographs) and "human time"

11. Steve Mirsky, *Scientific American* 287, no. 3 (September 2002), 102.

(measurable only subjectively through the most ancient of feelings: from fear to joy, from anxiety to boredom). Nonetheless time is an unsolvable enigma that every people, every culture, and every civilization has always attempted to represent (even by dabbling in astronomy). This drive was particularly strong in the Middle Ages: from the monk Werner Rolewinck, who printed a chronicle of the world in the form of a genealogical chart, to the geographer Peter Bienewitz, who invented a sort of astronomical computer with four boards with wheel charts.

There have even been attempts to dress time in architectural clothing. I'm thinking here of the Teatro della Memoria, which the Italian humanist Giulio Camillo Delminio described in his treatise *L'idea del theatro* (The Idea of the Theater), and which he perhaps was actually able to build partially, thanks to the support of Alfonso of Aragon. The work was a wooden construction directly inspired by the model in Vitruvius's *On Architecture*: it was made of seven columns each with seven rows, thus subdividing the entirety into forty-nine cells. Each cell was assigned, as a mnemonic device, a symbolic figure from mythology, the cabal, or hermeticism.

This "theater" was a sort of forebear to Aldo Rossi's *Teatro del Mondo* and Franco Purini's *Teatrino scientifico*, in which the spectator, sitting in the center of the stage, could look at each of the fields of universal knowledge and could memorize them thanks to their respective positions. It's this that Peter Eisenman hopes for when, thinking about the fate of the gaze in the era of electronic media, he accuses architecture of never having seriously faced up to the problem of *vision*, "that particular characteristic of sight which attaches seeing to thinking," both in architectural design and in architectural surveying.

> "Looking back" does not require the object to become a subject, that is, to anthropomorphize the object. "Looking back" concerns the possibility of detaching the subject from the rationalization of space. In other words, to allow the subject to have a vision of space that no longer can be put together in the normalizing, classicizing, or traditional construct of vision; an other space, where the space "looks back" at the subject. A possible first step in conceptualizing this "other" space, would be to detach what one sees from what one knows—the eye from the mind. A second step would be to inscribe space in such a way as to endow it with the possibility of looking back at the subject.[12]

Among Eisenman's experimental techniques of "looking back" on the anthropocentric subject, one that stands out is "scaling." In this technique, a series of computerized survey data (geographic, historic, metric, economic, geologic, aesthetic) that may be (but are not necessarily) relevant to the site's location are layered, sometimes with different scales, and combined with the principles of fuzzy logic. Indecipherable and apparently insignificant results emerge from these combinations, but in reality they are quite significant as they are tied to specific vagaries of that very spot and of the author of the scales.

It's much like Jackson Pollock's action painting, where different colors of paint were thrown on the canvas and only thereafter could the underlying compositional structure be "recognized." It's out of this iconic lump that intricate (and intriguing) layouts are born, in which the existing city is inter-

---

12. Peter Eisenman, *Written into the Void: Selected Writings, 1990–2004* (New Haven: Yale University Press, 2007), 35, 37.

preted as a territory in flux, where the boundaries between chance and causation are hard to define. It's the same with Eisenman's *Moving Arrows, Eros, and Other Errors: Romeo and Juliet*, an extremely experimental project not coincidentally presented at the Venice Biennale of 1985. Set in Verona, it involved a random superimposing of maps of the city—each of which embodied a rereading of the Shakespearian play set there—based on "discontinuity," on "revelation," and on "self-similarity." Out of these random overlays sprang a new urban form, invisible to the senses but visible to thought. This combination was rich with identity, as it was indissolubly linked to a particular expression of a place (the Verona of the Capulets and Montagues) and to a still more particular expression of the author of the overlay (Peter Eisenman). Ultimately, the beauty of our historic city centers is exactly that: we could never relocate (at least not easily) the picturesque neighborhood of San Pellegrino in Viterbo, or the "competing stratifications" of the Palazzo del Popolo in Ascoli Piceno. They are intimately connected and structured, through the recombinant processes of the various architectural additions, to the particularities of the *here and now*. Here we're getting to the heart of this lecture, though it requires one last digression.

Before I conclude this section, I'd ask you to use your imagination to fly into one of the halls of the Castle of Vaduz, where a mysterious painting is preserved that was executed in the first half of the sixteenth century by the Flemish painter Herman Posthumus. The painting gives the viewer the classic image of a chaotic mound of ruins, decomposing and sealed with the epigraph engraved on a sarcophagus in the foreground. This reads *Tempus edax rerum, tuque invidiosa vetustas, omnia destruitis*, "O Time, thou great devourer, and thou, envious Age, together you destroy all things"—a line from Ovid's *Metamorphoses* which celebrates the power of time to devour all things, beginning with monuments.

Not coincidentally, the left side of the scene is dominated by a path that winds up to the top of a small hill on which the ruins are close to being reabsorbed into nature. On the right, the ruins of a majestic temple stand out, with tall columns made from jasper covered with ivy and the vestiges of a barrel vault with plants growing all over it. In the background, behind a covered corridor and what seems to be a funeral monument, one can see the faded skyline of the Rome of Pope Paul III (1534–1549). So far there's nothing exceptional, as the passion for the picturesque was a sentiment common to most of the artists of that time.

Looking more attentively, you notice the unusual presence of a draftsman (seated on a toppled-over column in the foreground) who is intent on measuring the base of a column with a compass. A closer look reveals that it might be the same column to which Andrea Mantegna's St. Sebastian is bound, one which stands out against a background that is just as ruined. In that painting, an aqueduct with the space below its vaults used as workshops and a triumphal arch full of occasional, unplanned additions make up an architectural cross section. The abstract, Renaissance geometric rigor draws its expressive power from the complications of a city built and then dismantled, piece by piece, by time.

The city tends to creep outside the narrow perimeters of any theoretical superstructure artificially imposed by critics. We who are children of Donato Bramante and Andrea Palladio (two of the greatest architectural surveyors in history) should not have a hard time understanding the opportunity (and perhaps even the necessity) of not fixating on measuring the physical dimensions, but rather concentrating on the immaterial ones. We should appreciate the linkages of spatial juxtapositions and reconstruct the ways they developed, to the point of eliminating the boundaries between architectural survey and architectural design.

Just as illuminating, while we're on the subject, is the painting *Capriccio col Ponte di Rialto secondo il progetto del Palladio, la basilica di San Marco e uno scorcio di Palazzo Chiericati a Vicenza*, done around the middle of the seventeenth century by Giovanni Antonio Canal (better known as Canaletto). It's an eclectic montage in which, as explained by Aldo Rossi, "three Palladian monuments, none of which is actually in Venice (one is a project; the other two are in Vicenza), nevertheless constitute an analogous Venice formed of specific elements associated with the history of both architecture and the city." But what interests us most about Aldo Rossi's opinions on the painting is that "the geographical transposition of the monuments within the painting constitutes a city that we recognize, even though it is a place of purely architectural references."[13] So I would ask you: is the painting by Canaletto an informed act or an inventive one? That is to say, within its

---

13. Aldo Rossi, *The Architecture of the City* (Cambridge: Opposition Books, 1984), 166.

frame, which buildings are more important: the real ones, or the ones that existed only in the artist's imagination? If you've followed my line of reasoning, you won't hesitate to say that in Canaletto's work, it's not possible to distinguish what is knowledge from what is invention, what is real from what is fantasy.

I want you to begin to question the validity of a commonplace that is unfounded (though quite widely believed in academic circles). According to this idea, adding the variable of *time* in the architectural survey is a mere consequence of the digital revolution, allowing the creation of animated computer simulations. Too little, and too simplistic—because, as we've seen, there's a lot more to it than that.

5
Z_depth/interpretation

What I've said about the heuristic value of the architectural survey is valid whether our interpretation is *voluntary* (that is, guided by our biased glance) or *involuntary* (directed by what I would call "a perceptual misunderstanding"). On the other hand, it's incontrovertible that the subjectivity of the surveyor can influence the object of his survey, and that the object of the surveyor's gaze can be influenced by the subjectivity of the surveyor. Both come from the fallibility of human nature, which nudges us toward taking measurements that conform to our expectations while leading us to perceive reality based on what we know.

This principle gives substance to the object of the survey, increasing or decreasing its "depth" with respect to the xy plane. To clarify it, I think it's important to remind you that just like language, the symbols that drawing uses to communicate—which, as we've seen, are a fundamental component of the architectural survey—are the bearers of a message. It's an activity that theoretically should be deterministic but which in fact is not. The reason is that a "perceptual misunderstanding" gets between the emitter and the receiver. This misunderstanding can become habitual when the receiver isn't able to get a message different from what he expects, but it can also be creative when the receiver gets a message different from the one that was sent (and which can be just as meaningful, if not more so).

That was a mouthful: I'll try to explain myself with two examples, the first of which has to do with art (and with habitual misunderstanding), while the second has to do with archaeology (and with creative misunderstanding). First example: for centuries people have watched horses gallop, and they've made paintings and prints with horses leaping into battle or running behind bloodhounds. Nonetheless, no one seems to have ever noted how a horse *actually* gallops. Painters and engravers, bowing to common knowledge, had always represented them with their hooves stretched out, almost balanced in the movement of their stride. The French painter Théodore Géricault immortalized horses running in just this way in a famous painting in the Musée du Louvre in Paris (*Course de chevaux*, better known as *Le derby de 1821 à Epsom*).

Then a hundred years ago, a dramatic turning point. The camera had reached a degree of perfection such that it could provide stop-action photographs of horses running, and it was unequivocally shown that painters and the general public were wrong. No horse had ever launched itself in a gallop in the way that had always seemed natural to us. The truth is that the horse alternately folds its hooves underneath it as it takes them off the ground, and it's clear that it could not do otherwise. Despite that, when painters started to make use of this discovery, drawing horses running as they do in reality, everyone criticized them and their works were considered incorrect.

A second example: several years ago, Farouk El-Baz (director of the Center for Remote Sensing at Boston University) advanced a novel hypothesis about the origin of the pyramids and of the Egyptian sphinxes, an origin based on a creative misunderstanding. According to his theory, certain tribes of nomads crossing the oasis of Kharga around 3000 BCE were struck by the landscape of Egypt's Western Desert. That part of the desert is dotted with chalk outcroppings sculpted by the elements: these geological formations resemble pyramids and petrified lions, so much so that they could be interpreted as supernatural displays. These tribes, intermarrying with the communities already living in the Nile valley, introduced their sacred icons, among them the "pyramidal hill" and the "crouching lion." These phenomena generated by erosion are not exclusively found in that desert, but—if we give some credence to El-Baz's fascinating hypothesis—only the Egyptian nomads (perhaps in virtue of the attitude toward abstraction of "uncivilized thought") were capable of looking at them with a poetic eye.

It's not hard to understand that the biggest fans of creative misunderstanding (and with it, of serendipity) are artists. An example is Jeff Wall, whose lens has always been attracted to chance made manifest on the set. How could we not think of a shot entitled *Morning Cleaning*, in which a janitor is immortalized while listlessly going about his daily tasks? This act in and of itself would have been insignificant, had it not happened while Wall was busy with a photo shoot for the renovation of the pavilion built by Mies van der Rohe in Barcelona in 1929. In *Morning Cleaning*, the pavilion is shown quite differently from the cold images published on the glossy pages of books on architectural history: the pavilion is bathed in the morning's first sunlight, and the Barcelona chairs (usually precisely lined up against the walls) are all out of place. The red curtains are gathered together in a corner and the glass wall is covered with soapy water which obscures the statue *Amanecer* by Georg Kolbe (normally in plain sight). The same thing happened to the composer Gioacchino Rossini. In a letter addressed to Louis Engel (and published by W. H. Auden in *The Dyer's Hand and Other Essays*), Rossini admitted without a hint of false modesty the fortuitous inspiration for one of the main movements of the opera *Mosè in Egitto*:

> When I was writing the chorus in G Minor, I suddenly dipped my pen into the medicine bottle instead of the ink; I made a blot, and when I dried it with sand (blotting paper had not been invented then) it took the form of a natural, which instantly gave me the idea of the effect which the change from G minor to G major would make, and to this blot all the effect—if any—is due.[14]

---

14. W. H. Auden, *The Dyer's Hand and Other Essays* (New York: Random House, 1990), 16.

It's impossible not to agree with Auden when, wanting to laud the sincerity of Rossini, he decides that "such an act of judgment, distinguishing between Chance and Providence, deserves, surely, to be called an inspiration." From this point of view, architecture is certainly not an exception, as it manifests a notable inclination (bordering on passion) for planned creative misunderstanding. For example, when Raphael drew the interior of the Pantheon, he didn't produce "the reality one sees," but rather made some slight variations in the placement of the columns which "opened" the walls, giving back "the reality which should be seen." It was a ploy as simple as it was effective.

It's not a coincidence that the critical reception of this drawing (perhaps one of the most imitated in the history of architecture) is not imposed by its documentary rigor but rather by the spatial impression created in the observer. The same thing happened when the architect Andrea Palladio visited Assisi: he didn't care about the monastery complex but rather concentrated on the Temple of Minerva. This choice too is a type of perceptive misunderstanding, habitual to the culture of the times. He ultimately didn't draw a survey, perhaps because of the time it would have cost an accomplished landscape architect. When he later inserted the plan and the perspective view of the front of the temple in the supplementary illustrations in the last volume of *The Four Books of Architecture*, he was forced to redraw a survey from a preexisting one, a survey which he immediately "corrected."

Indeed Palladio, despite remembering the steps present below the level of the bases of the pedestals, did not consider them consonant with a construction exemplary of the Roman era. He made up a stylobate above five steps around the pronaos—all out of thin air. This stylobate had never been there "in reality," but from that moment on it became "the reality." So much so that despite Giovanni Antolini's essay (written in the nineteenth century) revealing the truth of the matter, the huge diffusion of Palladio's treatise prevailed over the limited number of copies of Antolini's essay, giving imprecision a leg up over precision. The moral is simple: knowledge of the Pantheon in Rome and the Temple of Minerva in Assisi was steered by the creative misunderstandings knowingly perpetrated by Raphael and Palladio.

It was with just such a creative misunderstanding that Sebastiano Giannini, eighteenth-century editor of Francesco Borromini's *Opus architectonicum*, directed scholars to search for medieval elements in Borromini's architecture. Giannini, in his "cleaning up" of the cross section of the Roman church of Sant'Ivo alla Sapienza, introduced a geometric construction that he simply made up, the famous double triangle. Even today this is paraded around as a typically Borrominian element. Borromini's original drawing, preserved in the Albertina Library in Vienna, has only one triangle. All this cannot and should not surprise you, because in the past there was no mass tourism. Knowledge was driven (and therefore conditioned) by the few people who were able to afford the luxury of travel, and by the even fewer who were able to find the resources to publish (and therefore spread) their own drawings.

Indeed, these often were very much approximations, so much so that it led Carlo Fontana, in the first book of *Templum Vaticanum*, to distance himself from the work of the improvising surveyors. He laid claim to the skills of a trade that, in addition to recording a building's characteristics, is also called upon to guard its memory in the (unfortunate) event of its loss:

> The great buildings must be described, and shown, by knowledge-able architects, historians, and those who practice similar disciplines, in order that most truly and with the appropriate terms their singular qualities can be brought to light, and can be manifested not only to peoples not able to see them, by reason of the distance of their countries, but also to our descendants who, with this text and illustrations, will be able to comprehend all the parts and measures even when the same might be destroyed, either by the voracious-ness of time or by other causes.[15]

The problem then is exquisitely hermeneutic, in the sense that we have to stop and ask ourselves a question when we find a historic document in our hands—for example, a drawing of a medieval church done by a young northern European aristo-crat while on the Grand Tour. We should ask ourselves whether it's correct to study it with today's eyes, filtering with a cultural sieve that (evidently) belongs only to us and our age. Perhaps not. Maybe it would be better to ponder the knowledge and the interests of the document's author without disconnecting them from the sociocultural context of the intended viewers in the past. But to put together two aphorisms (the first attributed to Oscar Wilde, the second coined by David Hume): "beauty

---

15. Carlo Fontana, *Templum Vaticanum et ipsius origo*, Book I (Rome: Giovanni Francesco Buagni, 1694), 3.

doesn't express anything" because "beauty in things exists in the mind which contemplates them."

With this I'd like to object to Fontana's complaint and remind you that each of us, with our own particular inner being, can give different meanings to beauty. Beauty has aesthetic value precisely because it's not something certain and definite, but stimulates reflection. It allows each of us to take away or add what we most want, depending on our experience and our own thoughts.

In the years in which I taught in the Department of Architecture in the Second University of Naples, my students worked in the zone formerly known as the Terra di Lavoro (in the hinterland of Naples), surveying over two hundred courtyards spread between the towns of Villa di Briano, Casagiove, and Caivano. What they brought back was always exciting, both from the graphic point of view and from the textual one. That said, four of my students went above and beyond my best expectations. The survey assigned to them was northeast of the historic center of the city of Aversa, in the heart of a neighborhood called Borgo San Lorenzo, just a few dozen meters from the Benedictine monastery of San Lorenzo ad Septimum.

It was also just a few hundred meters from a highway interchange, and in any event in the middle of an urban zone that frustrated any attempt to distinguish between legality and illegality. It was a typical situation: a shantytown that persisted on the foundations of an age-old rural farmyard. Typical too was the atmosphere of a ramshackle habitat: a true ode to the temporary where there was nothing permanent. My students encountered the typical difficulty of pinning down, metrically and geometrically, that kind of structure—it's obviously hard in a shantytown to fix trustworthy points of reference. Their survey, though, did not leave out any of the classical elements: from the explanation of the method adopted to take measurements, to the graphic representations in various sections, to the building of a model in wood.

But that wasn't all. In this courtyard, the necessity of having someplace protected from the elements had led to the building of an improvised roof. As is typical of the do-it-yourself style of construction, the job had been done using recycled materials: streetlamp poles for the pillars, corrugated iron for the cladding, and sheets of asbestos for the covering. Evidently, though, the poles weren't tall enough, so an anonymous builder (identified by my students with the made-up name of "Uncle Michele") had fixed this with the most classic expedient possible in the art of the makeshift. That is, of course, by utilizing construction elements that are perhaps inappropriate, but are close at hand: some tire rims, a roll of rusty wire, and a piece of a belt previously used to hold up shutters.

This together was an extraordinary architectural invention—comparable in some ways to Jacques Carelman's *objets introuvables*—a column that the students, flying on the wings of enthusiasm, had immediately rebaptized the "sixth order." They took a step back later, changing the bombastic "sixth order" into a more modest "Aversan order," but they didn't give up playing at the margins between serious and facetious. With the irony typical of Neapolitans, intuition had been supported with metric (and stylistic) comparisons between the profiles of the five classical orders of columns (inspired by the *Homo humanus* of the Renaissance era) and the amended one of the "sixth order" (by *Homo technologicus* of the bionic era). The comparisons were only apparently over the top, because they were much like some of their illustrious precedents: the "rustic hut" of Abbé Laugier or the "tree column" of Philibert de l'Orme.

The "courtyard of the sixth order" was along the road I walked down every morning to go to the department, but before then I had never noticed its existence. Passing by that ramshackle courtyard, I started to understand that reality is always and in any event the fruit of an interpretive plan which represents the meeting point between analysis and intention; and therefore the survey, as Franco Purini said, is "the place par excellence where the desire to change the world changes the perception that we have of it." If you think about it, this means that the survey marks out the territory between the technique of imitating-interpreting and that of depicting-reproducing. The practice of the survey is well illuminated in the *Primo libro del Trattato delle perfette proporzioni* ("Treatise on Perfect Proportions," published in Florence in 1567). The author, Vincenzo Danti, doesn't hide his preference for imitating-interpreting:

> And for this reason one can say that copying is as different from imitating as the writing of history is from the making of poetry, as I have said above; and that the artist who uses imitation is as superior in nobility and in dignity to the copyist as the poet is incomparably nobler and on a higher level than the historian.[16]

---

16. Vincenzo Danti, "Of the Distinction that I Make between Imitation and Copying," excerpted in Robert Klein and Henri Zerner, *Italian Art, 1500–1600: Sources and Documents* (Englewood Cliffs, NJ: Prentice-Hall, 1966), 182.

That the practice of imitating-interpreting (in comparison to the practice of depicting-reproducing) demands creativity is seen in the clinical case of the "Crane Baby," analyzed at the end of the 1970s by the Canadian psychiatrist François Péraldi. David Leavitt later dedicated a whole chapter (not to mention the title) of his first novel to the story in *The Lost Language of Cranes*. There are three brief but intense pages about the baby, a veritable ode to the practice of imitation-interpretation. The protagonist of the narrative is Jerene, a young scholar who, while she's in the library doing research to finish her dissertation on "invented languages," almost accidentally stumbles upon an article which talks about Michel. This baby, the product of a rape, lived until he was two in a decrepit housing project located next to a huge construction site. His mother, burdened with work, always left him completely alone.

For some time the baby cried and shrieked at the top of his lungs, provoking the protests of the other residents of the building. Then one day he was silent. The neighbors, alarmed by the sudden silence, called social services which broke into the apartment and, to their great surprise, found the baby on his feet on the bed. He was intently observing the construction site out the window, imitating the movements and the noises of the huge construction cranes. The baby was taken from his mother and put in an institution for handicapped children, where he continued to move like a crane for the rest of his life, reacting only to photographs of cranes and playing only with models of cranes. Reading the article upsets Jerene, who begins asking herself a series of disconcerting questions.

What did it sound like? What did it feel like? The language belonged to Michel alone; it was forever lost to her. How wondrous, how grand those cranes must have seemed to Michel, compared to the small and clumsy creatures who surrounded him. For each, in his own way, she believed, finds what it is he must love and loves it; the window becomes a mirror; whatever it is that we love, that is who we are.[17]

It's a moving passage which moreover (to get to what is important for us here) makes the perfect connection, across six hundred years of history, between the "window-mirror" described by David Leavitt and the Florentine "window-mirror" set up by Filippo Brunelleschi in front of the Baptistery of San Giovanni Battista. Neither produced only knowledge, but both induced (perhaps above all) wonder, establishing new points of view and opening new cultural horizons. Where Brunelleschi enchanted spectators with the illusionistic value of his panel paintings, Leavitt charms his readers with the melancholy value of a language which was lost and incomprehensible.

The same with prehistoric art, incomprehensible (and thus lost in a way) to the scientific world of the late nineteenth century, or the way certain things are lost to us today (and are therefore incomprehensible). Think of the many objects that were once very familiar but have been burned on the altar of convenience and forgotten because of the increased speed of life: matches (replaced by lighters), postcards (supplanted by Facebook), and cuckoo clocks (made moot by digital chronometers). Do you think that if an architect—or an engineer, a surveyor, a building expert, professional titles that in my

---

17. David Leavitt, *The Lost Language of Cranes* (New York: Houghton Mifflin, 1997), 203.

opinion aren't important—were called upon to measure the kitchen of an apartment, she would put down her laser tape measure and pick up a watercolor brush? If the same architect were called to survey an anonymous design object, for example a coffee service, would she neglect to reconstruct its geometric profiles? Would she be interested in the hopes and disappointments of the people who have used it? I think, though, that a great architect-poet like Aldo Rossi could do it, giving us designs again that were able to evoke the boundary (full of nostalgia) between collective history and private experience. I'm thinking here of his domestic works like *Interno veneziano* and *Una lettera*, but also (even more relevant for what I just said) a "still life with architecture" like *Dieses ist lange her/Ora questo è perduto*.

I have very clear ideas about this, as I'm sure you've gathered. The activity of a survey architect, just like that of a design architect, cannot ever be done with inattention—and by that I mean placing one's faith in the automations of a rote procedure turned over to some sophisticated instrumentation—but rather requires great care and great sensitivity. Because, as Davide Vargas has written in one of his entertaining stories in *Racconti di architettura*, "Each drawing is a door. A flight. A gossamer flight from here to there."[18] Perhaps, for you as well, it's time to pay attention to the implicit invitation of the Albertian motto *Quid tum* ("What next?"), opening your eyes and trying to fly. Because, observing the great earthly backdrop of the "Theatrum Mundi" from above, you can see things in another way, letting you find solutions that were otherwise unthinkable.

---

18. Davide Vargas, *Racconti di architettura* (Naples: Casa Editrice Tullio Pironti, 2012), 48.

6

Does a Forest Give Up Its Secret if You Measure the Height of the Trees?

I don't want to bore you with theoretical lectures that might seem ineffectual, if not even unessential. I can see that you're anxious to pull out your 3D scanner and grab your mouse to "put reality in a cage" inside your AutoCAD files. But I also know that theory is fundamental for any applied science. Just as I know that theory doesn't simply come out of nothing, but rather has its roots in the abstraction of practical processes. In other words, if theory governs application, application also fosters theory, in a feedback loop that is continuous and progressive. It's a process moreover that constitutes the foundation of Western civilization.

This is already enough of a reason to talk about theories of representation and their application as a function of the continuing improvement of the same theories. Nevertheless, there's also another good reason for not underestimating theoretical aspects (perhaps more convincing than the first reason). It concerns our privileged position as children of humanism. We are heirs of a world which, with the creation of the first late-sixteenth-century academies (beginning with the one inspired by Giorgio Vasari), promoted the draftsman from *artifex* (artisan) to *inventor* (professor). This makes sense because it's precisely the capacity to theorize that distinguishes the scholar from the technician, recognizing those who practice a discipline as a scientific calling rather than simply as a profession.

Therefore it's theory, not practice, that gives a discipline an identity. It's not coincidental, then, that for an architectural surveyor there's a risk of letting technology lead you astray. This risk—confusing the means with the end—represents a true sword of Damocles which looms and will always loom over your heads, making you think that an architectural survey, to be worthwhile, has to be rigorous and precise. That rigor and precision may seem absolutely fundamental, inescapable to you. But there's nothing further from the truth!

Of course you might still believe in their importance if you think of the punctilious way with which Leon Battista Alberti, in his book *De statua* (On Statues), describes the *finitorium*. This book—along with Alberti's *De re aedificatoria* (On Building) and *De pictura* (On Painting)—make up the most important trilogy of Renaissance manuals on art. Alberti describes the use of the *finitorium*, a mechanical device positioned above the statue being surveyed; the example given in the book is the statue of Castor and Pollux of Montecavallo, in Rome. This *finitorium* has a circular disc with a rotating arm which has a weighted string hanging from it, making the survey of the statue's members much easier. Today we would use a 3D scanner, a device which almost magically annuls the four hundred years that separate the sixteenth-century "linear profiles" from the twenty-first-century "point clouds."

In any event the affirmation ("that an architectural survey, to be worthwhile, has to be rigorous and precise") becomes much less believable if you think about the typological (not metric) observations made by Pirro Ligorio during his architectural survey of the so-called Mura di Santo Stefano (near the Villa of Caius Caecilius in the countryside outside of Rome), which inspired him to invent the architectural principles of his proto-type of the "antiseismic house."

> Thus, therefore, the most secure in buildings are those arches of square blocks (and when they are doubled they are much better) above the doors, the windows, and the other openings, just as here I show in the drawing. Of aid too is the use of square blocks to reinforce the corner pilasters, as they close and hold together the corners of the walls. All of the walls made of Roman brick, or of terra cotta, made perpendicular, are the most resistant and the most stable, and resist better the impetuous clashes of large movements, and they are made to stand firm, these and the aforementioned arches, and therefore these arches resist and stand against recipro-cal percussions. In addition to Pliny, Vitruvius recommends them; and indeed one sees them in the ancient fabrications, in the Casa Augustana, in the Baths of Agrippa, in those of Nero, in those of Titus …, as in other remains of the excellent fabrications of Rome, and outside of it. The most secure then, in buildings, are arches above all the openings…. And the illustrious authors say that the walls of Roman brick receive less damage being then well connected…. And the Roman bricks remain in perpetuity, as they resist those said percussions and fire and time.[19]

But the previous affirmation ("that an architectural survey, to be worthwhile, has to be rigorous and precise") loses any believability if you think of the demystifying irony of Jorge Luis Borges in the one-paragraph-long short story "On Exactitude in Science." Borges transposes into literature the interesting paradox of Josiah Royce on the uselessness of an exact copy, condemning the excess precision of a map that is so rich with

---

19. Pirro Ligorio, *Libro, o Trattato de' diversi terremoti*, Ferrara, [1571], f. 59v (Archivio di Stato di Torino, Cod. Ja.II.15).

information that each point in the country corresponded exactly with its own image on the same map.

> In that Empire, the Art of Cartography attained such Perfection that the map of a single Province occupied the entirety of a City, and the map of the Empire, the entirety of a Province. In time, those Unconscionable Maps no longer satisfied, and the Cartographers Guilds struck a Map of the Empire whose size was that of the Empire, and which coincided point for point with it. The following Generations, who were not so fond of the Study of Cartography as their Forebears had been, saw that that vast Map was Useless, and not without some Pitilessness was it, that they delivered it up to the Inclemencies of Sun and Winters. In the Deserts of the West, still today, there are Tattered Ruins of that Map, inhabited by Animals and Beggars; in all the Land there is no other Relic of the Disciplines of Geography.[20]

In the end, in the field of architectural surveying, the use of the adjectives "rigorous" and "precise" (very dear to the enthusiasts of topography) risk seeming deceptive if not downright erroneous. Indeed, even if certain very particular types of architectural survey are, in order to be meaningful, the exact representations of the object surveyed (as in the survey of painted decorations, where the output could actually substitute for the original), the vast majority of possible types are ultimately representations that, precisely in order to be meaningful, must distance themselves from the object surveyed. Tourist maps often enlarge the dimensions of those streets more trafficked by cars and pedestrians, to show their importance. What's represented on the map then corresponds to the qualitative

20. Jorge Luis Borges, *Collected Fictions*, trans. Andrew Hurley (New York: Penguin 1999), 325.

dimension, not the quantitative. I'm thinking here especially of Via del Corso in Rome: it's a small street that on a map is as wide as an avenue.

The qualities of unique urban landmarks—for example the main square of Siena, the Piazza del Campo—elude any representation, however aided by numerous drawings. Neither detailed maps (even those capable of bringing to life the complexity of the geometric connections to the urban neighborhoods, the *contrade*) nor focused cross sections (despite being able to describe the flexibility of the conch-shell shape of the piazza), let alone theatrical drawings (despite being able to represent the uniformity of the tops of all of the buildings around the perimeter), will ever be able to transmit the magic of a cold drink sipped in the shade of the town hall's bell tower. Not to mention being able to capture the sounds and the colors that bring Siena's famous medieval horse race, the Palio, to life.

The fact is (and this is the leitmotiv of the course) that in architectural surveying, metric precision not only is not a discriminating factor, it's a variable. This in the sense that the scale of the measures always depends in any case on the ends the measurement is used for. I'll try to explain myself with three intentionally varied examples.

The first example: *The Englishman Who Went Up a Hill but Came Down a Mountain*, a movie directed by Christopher Monger in the early '90s, narrates the story of a small town in Wales at the beginning of the twentieth century. Proud of their mountain village, the townspeople mobilize themselves (and the seductive charm of Tara Fitzgerald) to raise the height of the peak that stands over the village. They have to increase the elevation by 20 feet in order to reach the decisive height of 1,000 feet to be classified as a "mountain" rather than a "hill" by the two English geographers (played by Hugh Grant and Ian Hart) charged with the task of the cartographic update. In the dramatic concluding sequence, the parson even has himself buried at the pinnacle to contribute, with his own remains, to the reaching of the goal before the geographers take the official measurement of the height of the former hill. In this case the order of magnitude of the survey is the fathom, equal to six feet.

Second example: Michelangelo's notes. As is well known, the artist personally selected the blocks of marble destined to become the raw material for his sculptures. During his visits to the quarries of Carrara, Pietrasanta, and Seravezza, he used to mark the chosen blocks with his own symbol (three linked circles inside of which were the initials of the quarryman), then take down their outlines and dimensions with scrupulous geometric surveys written with quick strokes in special notebooks. In this case, the order of magnitude was the Florentine foot, just short of two feet.

Third example: the Formula One Grand Prix of Malaysia, won in 1999 by the Ferrari drivers Eddie Irvine and Michael Schumacher. When the federal technical inspector in Sepang, Jo Bauer, measured the carbon deflectors on the team's two vehicles, he found that on both they were one centimeter smaller than the officially mandated size. The Ferrari cars were disqualified and the victory was won by forfeit by Mika Häkkinen and the McLaren team. Later the FIA Court of Appeals (meeting in Paris) overturned that ruling, upholding the argument of the defense based on a different way of measuring, done by engineer Adrian Newey. With the help of a laser, he showed that the missing width was not 10 millimeters but rather 8, and thus within the allowed tolerances (20 percent). In this case the order of magnitude of the survey is a fraction of a centimeter. The metric difference of the measures in my three examples, then, goes from six feet to less than an eighth of an inch, confirming what I had said: that in surveying in general (and definitely in architectural surveying), precision in measurement is not absolute but rather relative, in that it must be proportional to the reasons for measuring.

Pay attention, as this is important and will allow you to free yourselves from technological slavery. Are you convinced, for example, that the sophisticated electronic instrumentation transported by the NASA rover *Curiosity* (video cameras, mass spectrometers, neutron detectors, etc.) will provide images of the planet Mars more captivating than Peter Suschitzky's computer-generated ones in the film *Red Planet*?

In other words, do you really think that to really know a building well, metric precision is the determining factor? Probably many of you will lean toward answering yes, because many of you are convinced that precision is the prerequisite for understanding the sense of things. In reality, though, metric precision by itself has little meaning. Meaning often remains hidden behind things and behind the representations of things. To explain it with Claude Debussy, "Does a forest give up its secret if you measure the height of the trees? Is it not rather its immeasurable depth that sets the imagination in motion?"

Architectural surveying has to do almost by necessity with the registration of reality by symbols that induce both a drastic simplification and a perceptible manipulation with respect to everything that is believed to be an accurate representation; it's in the genetic code of an informed act that is by its nature selective.

There's a faded pen drawing, preserved in the Bibliothèque Inguimbertine in Carpentras, done by a chaplain from that region, Jérôme Maurand. Maurand had set sail with the pirate captain Ariadeno Barbarossa, and had noted the salient features of the city of Lipari. Lipari is on one of the Aeolian Islands near Sicily, and it was the object of the pirate fleet's blockade and siege in the first half of July 1544. Maurand's on-sight survey seems improvised, because he made it while perched precariously on the deck of a floating galley, but in reality it's attentive and well-considered. The surveyor signed his work with a laconic annotation: "Lipari is made thus."

This is nothing exceptional, given that Maurand's drawing was published together with the on-sight surveys of all the Mediterranean ports he visited during the voyage from the Antibes to Constantinople: from Ventotene to Pozzuoli, from Gallipoli to Zante, from Chios to Constantinople. What is perhaps exceptional is the nonchalance with which Maurand, to highlight the military strategies devised by Barbarossa and his lieutenants, changed the real appearance of the buildings in Lipari. He accentuated the jagged character of the port to heighten its defensive fragility and elongated the mole of the Convent of San Bartolo to underline the exposed location, given the imminent pillaging.

What we're left with is a sketch that is as eccentric as the one, just as improvised and liberal with respect to reality, done four hundred years later by the luminary of urban design Giuseppe Samonà. Samonà was working on environmental impact studies for the drafting of the city of Cefalù's building codes, and drew from the prow of a fishing boat on the water. His drawings emphasized the rise in elevation from sea to inhabited zone to fortress, to show the steplike composition, augment the profile of the Norman cathedral, and point out the role of the "landscape measurements."

I think that the parallel I'd like to draw between the sketches of Maurand and Samonà is more than eloquent, as the two drawings—though distant chronologically and culturally—have an arbitrariness in common, one that reveals the unavoidably biased character of the survey. This is because surveying, as an investigative act, is always subordinated to different ends: the account of a historic event in progress in the case of Lipari, an analysis of the landscape in the case of Cefalù.

On the other hand, if you can get past your preconceptions, you'll realize that it's precisely those biases transferred onto paper by Maurand and Samonà that make the architectural survey valuable. Indeed, even though both the drawings were done from the sea—and with simple instruments: a pen in Maurand's case and a pencil in Samonà's—while we're comfortably seated at a desk with powerful tools at our disposal (such as personal computers and sophisticated software like Google Earth), it would be difficult to reach the same level of precision. Difficult because in architectural surveying, what really counts is not the instruments with which we're equipped, but rather the ideas that whirl about in our heads and the feelings that make our hearts beat.

So Antoine de Saint-Exupéry advised us in that extraordinary adventure story that trained my generation, *The Little Prince*: "You can only see things clearly with your heart. What is essential is invisible to the eye." And here the circle of my reasoning closes, because it's perhaps exactly for this reason that our eyes are blind to the unexpected. We have to put aside every presumption of rationalizing the world that surrounds us, and rediscover the ability to look at it with our hearts.

Given that importance of looking with our hearts, I can't help thinking of the book of Kings, where Solomon asks for "understanding to discern judgment" and God gives him "a wise and an understanding heart." I began this lecture with an unusual citation from the Old Testament; I'll close with a quote that's just as unusual. It's taken from the book *Liber in gloria martyrum*. It's a hagiographic work that's almost unknown today, though once more than familiar to those in religious communities. The text is a manuscript by Gregory of Tours written about 590 CE and dedicated to the celebration of the miracles attributed to the early Christian martyrs. Since you are certainly not required to know Latin (least of all its medieval version), I'll sum it up briefly for you. The story is about a miracle prayed for by a country priest and conceded by St. Lawrence, fixing an error made in the measurements for one of the wooden beams for the roof of a church dedicated to the saint. What's curious is that the length of the beam goes from one excess to another:

first it's too short, and then it's miraculously too long. I think that the anecdotal value of the story (at least from our point of view as enthusiasts of the architectural survey) is to show that metric precision is not necessarily an advantage.

And with it, that metric imprecision is not necessarily bad. First of all because, according to the story of the miracle of St. Lawrence, metric precision belongs neither to the earthly sphere (the parishioners who cut the beam too short) not to the celestial one (the saint who made the beam too long). But above all because the metric imprecision, again following the story of the miracle, is the source of happiness. Indeed, as written in the *Sincere Acts of the First Martyrs of the Catholic Church* by Francesco Maria Luchini, confronted with the excessive generosity of the saint, "they did not waste the leftover piece" of the beam because the faithful noticed that, after they got over their amazement, "they cut off small pieces of this, which often banished grievous infirmities." Finally, a happy ending!

I want to leave you with a positive message, taken from a unique didactic experience. I'm referring to an architectural survey done at the end of the 1960s by Robert Venturi, Denise Scott Brown, and Steven Izenour, together with a group of students from Yale University's School of Art and Architecture. This survey was made famous in their celebrated book *Learning from Las Vegas*, which opens with an affirmation surprising for that time:

> Learning from the existing landscape is a way of being revolutionary for an architect. Not the obvious way, which is to tear down Paris

and begin again, as Le Corbusier suggested in the 1920s, but another, more tolerant way; that is, to question how we look at things.[21]

As soon as it was published, the book unleashed sarcastic reviews and incited a controversy that was at times biting. Then, in just a few years, the most hostile detractors realized that their critiques were baseless. In the end, Venturi, Scott Brown, and Izenour, as university professors, had simply decided to update their studies, moving their attention from New York's Fifth Avenue and the National Mall in Washington to the Strip in Las Vegas: a virtual street (made of lights, sounds, and fake facades) in a city even more virtual, having sprung up in the heart of the Mojave Desert. Perhaps what had seemed foreign to the detractors wasn't the object of the study, but rather the method.

To survey the gigantic statues and huge neon signs, the team led by Venturi and Scott Brown had set aside the conventional tools (pencil, plumb line, tape measure, etc.) and, following the pioneering example of Michelangelo Antonioni in the film *Zabriskie Point*, adopted others that were seemingly eccentric (microphones, tape recorders, movie cameras, etc.). In reality they were appropriate, as they were able to capture the cacophonous soundtrack and the figurative trivialities of a city-mirage never before seen on the face of the earth, thrown up in the shortest of times, and decked out in the guise of a trade fair of the new commercial vernacular: from fast food to drive-in, from service station to shopping mall. The project mercilessly exposed the inadequacies of the architectural

21. Robert Venturi, Denise Scott Brown, and Steven Izenour, *Learning from Las Vegas: The Forgotten Symbolism of Architectural Form*, rev. ed. (Cambridge, MA: MIT Press, 1977), 3.

renderings (plan, section, and elevation) in the face of the sudden arrival on the urban scene of new phenomena like sprawl and junkspace.

> The representation techniques learned from architecture and planning impede our understanding of Las Vegas. They are static where it is dynamic, contained where it is open, two-dimensional where it is three-dimensional—how do you show the Aladdin sign meaningfully in plan, section, and elevation, or show the Golden Slipper on a land-use plan? Architectural techniques are suitable for large, broad objects in space, like buildings, but not for thin, intense objects, like signs…. We need techniques for abstracting, for example, to represent "twin phenomena" or to demonstrate concepts and generalized schema—an archetypal casino or a piece of the urban fabric—rather than specific buildings. The pretty photographs that we and other tourists made in Las Vegas are not enough.[22]

These days, despite the huge success of sites like Flickr and Pinterest, beautiful photos are no longer enough to describe cities that are traditionally photogenic like Venice or Paris. There's a need for more. "More" that, for a draftsman, doesn't have to do with either the picturesque views of street painters or the spot height maps cited by topographers. But it has to do with architectural surveying, especially if this can go beyond the narrow boundaries of technique and trespass into the artistic sphere, letting us see the things right under our noses but which, due to our insensitivity or our distraction, we haven't seen or (worse yet) can't see.

22. Ibid., 106.

To start seeing them (or to be able to again), we have to be like Hamlet when, waiting for the specter of his father, he condemns rational thought without pity: "There are more things in heaven and earth, Horatio, / Than are dreamt of in your philosophy." As always, the Shakespearian moral is obvious: with philosophy (but also with science) we try to speculate on the origin of the world and explain every aspect of life, but we miss things if we give up on irrational knowledge. There are many more things "seeable" with irrational knowledge than we can comprehend with rational thought.

The *Vision of St. Augustine*, painted by Filippo Lippi in the middle of the fifteenth century, seems to want to remind us of this. In it we see a baby who is taking water out of the sea with a shell. According to the legend, when St. Augustine asked him why he was doing this, the baby (who was really an angel) answered that the human attempt to understand the mystery of the Trinity (to which the saint had been dedicating himself in his writings) was as vain and impossible as trying to take all the water out of the ocean with a shell. Perhaps then, instead of trying to be able to know the absolute (poorly), we should be happy to know its simulacra (well). Just as Novalis (then named Georg Friedrich Philipp Freiherr von Hardenberg) advised us to do with his consideration of the paradox of determinism and experimentalism: "Everywhere we seek the Absolute, and always we find only things." Interestingly enough, even though this formulation is pregnant with meaning, the reverse is even more so.

How many of us search everywhere for the Absolute, concentrating our energies on fundamental problems, yet end up inevitably confusing theory with practice? And how many of us "find only things" at the moment when we think we are unifying the results of our treatises, giving them an overarching theoretical framework—all the while risking finishing up in the dustbins of prefab ideology? Given that, the academic spat stirred up by Novalis seems to lead us to a dead end. But it's not so, because, luckily for us, there's an alternative in the empirical action recommended by Confucius, according to which "the superior man is modest in words but excels in deeds." In that sense, picking up the thread again of the parallel tracks of drawing and writing created by the duet-duel between De Fiore and Hohenegger, we can't help noticing the uselessness of adding yet another chapter written in our own hand.

At best if we really want to say something new, we can modify the sense of something written by those who came before us. We can work on the punctuation or make strategic edits with erasures or additions in the white spaces that separate one word from another—and even this is only possible if we know the original text inside and out, or (getting back to architecture) if we know the existing building extremely well, something that is neither simple or immediate. But luckily you have precious opportunities to practice right now. Which ones? Those offered to you by a course on the Architectural Survey, of whose importance this lesson has tried to convince you.

Index

113